NAMIBIA
THE UNTAMED LAND

Gerald Cubitt

NAMI

Namibia is an uncompromising land of
by fierce climatic extremes. In the interior, frosty
droughts may be broken by torrential
accentuating the bleakness on one of the world's most desola
and en

NIBIA

THE UNTAMED LAND

e-inspiring landscapes carved from primordial rock formations
ck-shattering nights can follow scorching days; and long aching
ods. Along the coast, thick fogs move regularly in off an icy sea,
hores. It is a land of contrast; of wild rugged mountain ranges
ss flat plains, of formidable deserts and lush tropical swamps.

Relatively little of Namibia's land surface is suitable for permanent hu
Namib, a coastal desert encompassing over 150 000 square kilometres, contains so
regions of this vast land, for considerable parts of the more favoured country ha

Because of the broad spectrum of habitats that occur within Namib
most of the north, being particularly plentiful in the Etosha National Park and the
point of extinction, black rhinos in Etosha are thriving and have recently increa
ranging from the giant 1 200 kg giraffe to the tiny Damara dikdik whose weight av
jackals, foxes, aardwolf, badger and numerous smal
However, it is not only the magnificence of this big game t

On three sides Namibia is bounded by water
significantly harnessed within the country's borders
Namibia's many anomalies that onl

On a map it will be seen that numerous wandering blue lines also
for along their sandy courses water flows for just a few days, or at most weeks
'come down', but when they c

Although the larger seasonal rivers seldom actually contain r
available in abundance just beneath the sands. Periodically this subterranean wa
that trickle briefly over the smooth grey rocks or golden sa
widely scattered artesian springs, have played a vital role in the ecology of

Of the total land surface of Namibia, only about one fifth has an a
teak, kiaat, mopane and others that form endless dry forests stretching
swampland system on the subcontinent — a vast sea of *Phragmites* and *Papyr*
w

Above all, however, Namibia is a desert land, where o
benevolence of the seasons. In high rainfall years the fecundity of the
starvation and thirst stalk the land, harvesting, often with interest, the bounty
by capricious elements and, possibly because death is alwa

Today much of the old Namibia has been changed at the han
the strong heady essence of this harsh land is as potent and intoxicatin
ranges and awesome canyons mock man's

habitation, and today large tracts are still but lightly touched by the hand of man. The
of the most spectacular wilderness left on Earth. But wild areas are not confined to arid
so been set aside as national parks, game reserves and conserved recreational areas.

le land supports an exceptional variety of wildlife. Elephant are still found throughout
rivi Strip. While at a time when they are being persecuted in many parts of Africa to the
ramatically. A further twenty six distinct species of hooved game animals occur here,
s less than six kilograms. Lion, leopard, cheetah, wild dog, spotted and brown hyena,
nimal species can also be encountered in one or more of the country's natural regions.
as given Namibia its singular character, but also the rugged grandeur of the land itself.

ıding some of the largest rivers in Southern Africa, but to date none of them have been
heir influence on the land is restricted to the breadth of their floodplains. It is just one of
w kilometres from the banks of these mighty rivers the land is parched and waterless.

ate from the high central plateau, but these represent rivers that are such in name only,
ing the year. In times of drought many consecutive years may pass before these rivers
ey can be transformed within minutes into raging torrents that sweep all before them.

ng water, the magnificent trees that line their banks clearly indicate that water is, in fact,
s forced upwards by rocky obstructions in the river course, creating sparkling streams
before once more sinking beneath the surface. These little riverine streams, along with
and, for they form the focal points around which the game and early settlers gathered,
and without them much of the country would have been uninhabitable.

ge annual rainfall of more than 400 millimetres. In this favoured region tall trees grow:
nterruptedly to table-flat horizons. Within, this region is also part of the most extensive
Nymphaea waterlilies and islands of palms — that is fed by a complex network of
ways, some of which may flow in opposite directions at different times of the year.

ghts are almost predictable in their regularity, and the tempo of life is attuned to the
plains is remarkable; but inevitable lean years follow and soon the grim spectres of
nore benign seasons. Animal populations explode and are then quickly decimated
o close at hand, life here sometimes seems more exuberant than in milder climes.

f man, but the primordial grandeur of its natural scenery cannot be despoiled, and
ever. The mighty rivers on the borders surge onward unsubdued; the stark rugged
y monuments, and over all a fierce brooding spirit reigns, relentless and untamed.

Garth Owen-Smith

Opening illustrations:
The Spitzkoppe, a massive granite inselberg that
rises dramatically 600 metres above the
surrounding plains.

The world's largest dunes occur at Sossusvlei in
the central Namib desert.

Right: Full moon over the desert coast.

Previous page: Late afternoon sunlight
mellows the rugged western slopes of the Brandberg,
at 2 568 metres the highest mountain in Namibia.

Left: *Acacia mellifera* (subspecies *detinens*)
in full blossom brings a brilliant splash of colour
to the northern bushveld before the
onset of summer rains.

Following pages:
Sunset in the Etosha National Park.

The palm-fringed banks of the Kunene River
provide a striking contrast to the desolate
mountains along Namibia's north-west border.

An elephant herd moves leisurely through
sandveld savanna, a landscape that characterises
much of Caprivi.

FOR JANET —
who has shared with me
the heat and dust of
many weeks of travel in the
endeavour to portray
this magnificent country.

Published by Don Nelson, P.O. Box 859, Cape Town
ISBN 0 909238 65 0
Copyright text Garth Owen-Smith
Copyright photography Gerald Cubitt
Designed by Benni Hotz
Lithographic reproduction and typesetting by Hirt & Carter (Pty) Ltd., Cape Town
Printed and bound by C.T.P. Book Printers, Cape Town
First edition 1981
Second Impression 1985

BD3670

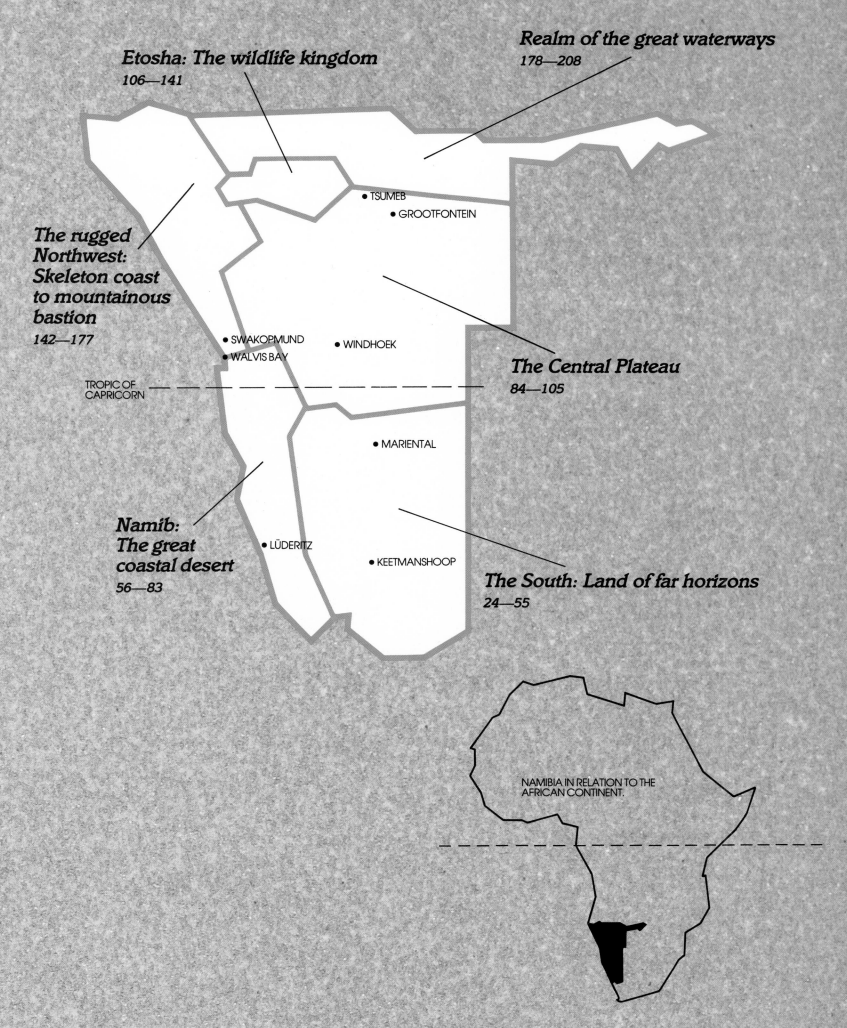

Etosha: The wildlife kingdom
106—141

Realm of the great waterways
178—208

The rugged
Northwest:
Skeleton coast
to mountainous
bastion
142—177

TSUMEB
GROOTFONTEIN

SWAKOPMUND
WALVIS BAY
WINDHOEK

TROPIC OF
CAPRICORN

The Central Plateau
84—105

MARIENTAL

Namib:
The great
coastal desert
56—83

LÜDERITZ

KEETMANSHOOP

The South: Land of far horizons
24—55

NAMIBIA IN RELATION TO THE
AFRICAN CONTINENT.

23

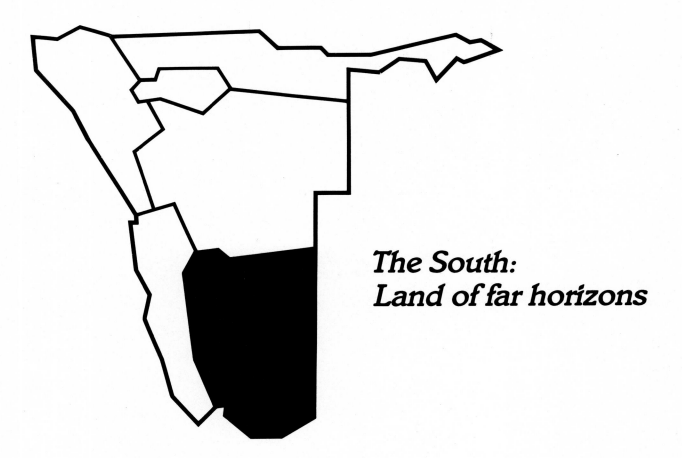

The South: Land of far horizons

On a vast landscape a band of men strides purposefully beside a small wagon. In their wake follow long-horned pack oxen and scruffy fat-tailed sheep, urged onwards by the staccato crack of rawhide whips and showers of damnation from dry, weather-beaten lips. On all sides the plains are parched — burned off to gravel and stone by endless days of searing heat — and a fine choking dust rises from the hooves of the gaunt beasts to hang like a pall in the still evening air. In the western sky a smouldering sun sinks slowly below a distant horizon, igniting dark banks of barren clouds that blaze briefly in a fierce conflagration of scorching colour.

Against the immensity of its setting, the straggling column is dwarfed into insignificance, but stout hearts beat within these breasts and already their tracks have been lightly etched onto nearly two thousand kilometres of pristine African veld. The direction of the march is northwards: ahead lie uncharted deserts and unnamed mountain ranges, high adventure, discovery and more than one close encounter with disaster. The year is 1837, and the man who leads this determined company of explorers is Captain James Alexander, the first European to travel overland from Cape Town to Walvis Bay — an epic journey that would, more than any other, bring to an end the old era in Namibia.

The south of Namibia is still today a harsh and unforgiving region of impassable mountain ranges and mighty river gorges, where water is nowhere plentiful and fearsome extremes of temperature can quickly sap the will and snatch the lives of the imprudent. For these pioneers there was not the comfort of maps or even sure waterholes. They trekked off into the unknown, relying on their ingenuity and unbounded faith to see them through.

To be sure, the trails they blazed would often have passed over the softer footprints of uncovered feet that wandered lightly over the sun-baked plains, following the great herds of game. Occasionally they might also have crossed the deeper imprints of leather sandals intermingled with the clustered spoor of herds and flocks that ranged near some of the permanent springs. Although the men that made these tracks had already been here for centuries, their impact on the ancient landscape was minimal, for they were at one with nature and lived in harmony with her fecundity and her famine; but in Alexander's footsteps came a new breed of men — men who were driven by a desire to conquer and place their stamp upon the land.

Inexorably, the winding game paths were replaced by arrow-straight roads and the plains were crisscrossed by ubiquitous wire fences. Much of the big game that Alexander encountered has also gone, its place taken by sleek herds of exotic cattle, karakul sheep and stubbornly independent farmers. Yet in spite of this, the bold scenery of the south has retained its ancient splendour; for against the scale of the Fish River Canyon, the Naukluft and the jagged ranges along the Orange River, man's enterprises have been but small indeed.

From the air the flat horizonless plain in the South seems to merge imperceptibly into an unblemished pale blue African sky. Periodically small dark ranges stretch the taut skin of the land like jutting bones on a wasted body. The earth appears old here, its surface faded and dulled by exposure to countless millennia of searing sun and desiccating winds.

The scorched red plains are pocked by salt-whitened pans and cicatriced by shallow water-courses, their dry channels marked by thin lines of scrubby grey bushes. Occasionally there are larger rivers, their broad beds fringed with taller trees whose dark green leaves bring some verdure to the

otherwise overwhelmingly colourless scene. In mid-summer, when the acacias are in bright yellow flower and emerald grass grows alongside the pale river sands, these larger water-courses look like sparkling ribbons threaded through the sunburned veld.

Along the south eastern borders serried ranks of red sand dunes extend across the flat steppes from neighbouring Botswana. These ancient outliers of the Kalahari are now immobile, stabilized by a tawny mane of Bushman grasses and scattered camel-thorn trees, but wherever this protective cover has been removed by overgrazing, the restless sands resume their slow advance westwards.

Not all of the south is flat. Between Keetmanshoop and Mariental lies Mount Brukkaros, a massive, long-extinct volcanic cone that towers 800 metres above the surrounding plains; while northwards towards the high central plateau gaunt brooding ranges become increasingly frequent. However, it is in the west, and particularly the south west, that this region reveals its most rugged countenance. At first the flat landscape is broken only by loosely-piled heaps of shiny black boulders that are strewn across the veld as if dumped at the site of a planned mountain range; but as one progresses further, the land surface wrinkles into badlands of broken hills and incised riverbeds that grade into the rocky ramparts of the Groot and Klein Karasberge. Beyond them is the great gaping canyon of the Fish River, a chasm second in size only to the Grand Canyon in North America.

Here is exemplified the awesome eroding power of water and time: from a dramatic quartzite cliff, scree slopes cascade in a wild jumble down to the river bed more than 600 metres below.

The Fish River Canyon portrays many moods of vivid contrast as the day progresses. The intensity of the light and the moving shadows create a continually changing perspective, so that the same scene just after sunrise and at mid-day is quite different. In the evening, when the folding ranges turn turquoise blue with deep dark shadows, the canyon is completely unrecognisable from the soft surreal pink and grey highlights that provided its early-morning mystique. To view the Fish River Canyon by the light of a full moon is to be transported back in time to an age before life existed on this planet. An immense silence permeates the senses and in the depths below the ghostly shadows speak of aeons of lifeless antiquity.

West of the canyon and north of the Orange River lie the rugged and virtually unexplored Hunsberge. Apart from the remote ranges in the northern Kaokoveld, the Hunsberge are the least-known mountains in Namibia; and since the German colonial period, there are no records of anyone having penetrated the range to any depth.

In all likelihood there are permanent springs in the Hunsberge as yet unrecorded, exciting speculation about the wildlife which would visit them. The southernmost natural population of Hartmann's Zebra (*Equus zebra hartmannae*) occurs here and there are also kudu, klipspringer and leopards on the remote, craggy slopes. Near Rosh Pinah at the western end of the range, farmers claim sightings of mountain reedbuck, a species not recorded elsewhere in Namibia.

The Hunsberge are situated in unallocated State land, but government approval has already been granted for the purchase of private property lying between these mountains and the Fish River Canyon Park in order to create a single conserved area nearly 450 000 hectares in extent, which would protect some of the most spectacular arid scenery in Southern Africa.

The stark, rugged scenery of south western Namibia has been carved from the ancient rock formation by a hostile and uncompromising climate. For nine months of the year the sun reigns supreme, blistering boulders and savagely desiccating the gnarled scrubby vegetation. Between Viools Drift and Goodhouse in the Orange River Valley day temperatures frequently exceed 45°C in the shade, making it possibly the hottest permanently inhabited place in the world. At noon here, the exposed black rocks become so hot that one can fry an egg on them, and in mid-summer the tar has been known to melt on the main road through Viools Drift.

The elements appear to have a particular vendetta against all who dare to live in this part of Namibia for in winter the region is regularly lashed by icy winds that sweep through the mountain passes and across the broad treeless plains, rattling the framework of the inhabitants' simple dwellings and the teeth of all who venture beyond the shelter of their homesteads. Even when the wind is still, the nights in June and July can be bitterly cold, with temperatures often falling well below freezing point. Aus, a lonely village set in bold granite hills on the edge of the southern Namib, has the distinction of being the only place in Namibia to record significant falls of snow.

In southern Namibia rainfall is by nature capricious and miserly, for in the far south and west precipitation is generally less than 100 mm per year, and even in the more favourable north-east of the region, the annual rainfall seldom exceeds 250 mm. Coupled with the devastating summer heat, this creates an extremely hostile environment for living organisms, but the hardy plants and animals have evolved in adversity: they ask little to flourish and can survive on much less. Only 100 mm of rain, if it falls regularly and at the right time of year, is suffcient to transform the parched plains into a sea of waving grass that can stretch unbroken from horizon to horizon.

Although rain falls mainly in the form of short summer or autumn storms, cloudy days with drizzle also occur, particularly in the far south and west, during any season. If good autumn rain is followed by heavy winter showers the drab and desolate veld is capable of a remarkable transformation as fast growing annuals burst into a bright carpet of blossoms that, in favourable years, can rival the world-famous wild flowers of Namaqualand. Some of the most spectacular displays occur in the rugged mountainous crescent between Warmbad and Aus, where countless succulents on the rocky slopes of the stark ranges bloom in a profusion of brilliant purple, pink, orange, red and yellow flowers.

In arid areas most plants appear to spend an extravagant amount of energy on flower production. Indeed, when heavy rain falls, many species produce a floral display out of all proportion to the size of the plant. Tiny mesembryanthemums, only a few centimetres high, bear large gawdy blossoms that dwarf the parent plant, while many of the larger shrubs adorn themselves with such a mass of blossom that the rest of the plant is barely visible.

As with all things in nature, there are sound reasons for such behaviour. In this harsh environment, where rainfall is unseasonal and erratic, the majority of plants match their flowering to the occurrence of rain and not to a particular time of year. Consequently, after a heavy downpour many different species come into bloom simultaneously, creating a situation of fierce competition between them for the attention of bees and other pollinators.

Because bees are relatively scarce in low rainfall regions, a number of plants depend instead on flies and carrion-eating beetles for pollination, attracting them with flowers that give off an odour of putrid meat. In a few Stapeliad species the large blooms even resemble pieces of rotting flesh.

The relative frequency of winter rainfall in south-western Namibia has created a habitat that is ideally suited to the growth of succulents, a group of plants characterised by fleshy leaves or stems, a feature that often gives them a strange and sometimes grotesque shape. The fleshy tissue in succulents is used to store fluids with which the plant is able to maintain its metabolic activities during long periods when the surface soil is devoid of water. Generally, succulents also have well developed superficial root systems which enable them to absorb soil moisture efficiently after even the lightest shower of rain, thereby replenishing the fluid stored within their leaves or stems.

During prolonged droughts, when no rain at all may fall for many months, the succulents' once-bloated storage organs gradually shrivel up until only a wrinkled cuticle remains. However, as long as there is still some fluid within the plant body, it is capable of a quick and quite remarkable recovery when rain falls once again.

The stored fluids on which succulent plants depend in order to survive would obviously be an attraction to the animal inhabitants of arid areas, and consequently these plants have had to evolve various adaptations to discourage browsers. Common deterrents include bitter or poisonous sap, and sharp spines that cause severe irritation when they penetrate the skin.

Probably the most extraordinary tactic, however, is the cryptic colouration employed by a group of small mesembs, whose markings and shape so resemble inanimate objects in their natural habitats, such as stones, pebbles, gravel and even coarse sand, that they escape the attention of thirsty herbivores.

In the south, twelve Aloe species occur, including three that grow into fairly large trees — *Aloe dichotoma, A. pillansii* and *A. ramosissima*. In years gone by Bushmen prized out the fibrous pith from pieces of tree aloe branch and used these tubes for quivers in which to carry their poisoned arrows. This practice has given these beautiful aloes their common name of Quiver Tree, *kokerboom* in Afrikaans.

Perhaps one of the most characteristic sights in southern Namibia is the sociable weavers' nest in a *kokerboom* or spreading camel-thorn tree. Sociable weavers are themselves rather nondescript grey-brown birds little bigger than sparrows,

but they live and breed in huge colonies, constructing enormous communal nests: one of the wonders of the animal kingdom. Made almost entirely from straw, a particularly large nest may extend 5 metres across and contain a hundred or more separate compartments where the little birds roost throughout the year and breed whenever conditions are favourable.

For protection, the openings to the individual brood chambers are all at the bottom of the nest facing downwards, but nevertheless snakes such as the Cape cobra and boomslang have little difficulty in getting into them, and may consume many of the nestlings and eggs as well as an occasional adult bird. Honey badgers may do even greater damage to the colony, for these tenacious predators sometimes climb into the tree and claw a nest to pieces in order to reach the young birds.

Sociable weaver nests are also used for roosting and breeding by a number of other birds, including the pygmy falcon, a small raptor that strangely does not appear to molest the weavers. In fact the presence of a pygmy falcon pair may actually be beneficial to their hosts for they prevent smaller egg-eating snakes from taking up residence in the nest. Rosy-faced lovebirds and various small finches are also known to breed in these convivial stacks of straw.

Before the large-scale introduction of firearms, big game was plentiful in southern Namibia. In 1760 Jacobus Coetzee, the first European to cross the lower Orange River, obtained permission from the Governor of the Cape to hunt elephant there, and although he shot only two of these animals, during a subsequent expedition under Willem van Reenen, a total of 65 rhinoceros, 6 giraffe and large numbers of other animals were killed north of the Orange.

In 1837 explorer James Alexander colourfully recorded that "lions were everywhere found . . . two-horned rhinoceros, both black and white, are found in the upper reaches of the Fish River; zebras are everywhere in the land; beautiful spotted panthers; plenty of giraffe or camelleopards, buffaloes, doodo's, gemsboks, elands, hartibeests, klip-springers, springboks and other of the deer tribe; hyenas, wild boars, jackals, polecats, rats and mice, are in great abundance." With regard to elephant, he wrote that by that time they already only occurred "several days' journey east of the Fish River".

Less than a century later Shortridge, author of the first standard reference on the mammals of Namibia, found that elephant, rhinoceros, giraffe and buffaloes had all disappeared from the south and that lion were restricted to the edge of the Kalahari and around the Naukluft mountains. However, not all of the big game animals have been exterminated: leopard and mountain zebra still occur in the more inaccessible ranges, while kudu, gemsbok and springbok survive on the properties of conservation-conscious farmers. Cheetah and jackal, which are ruthlessly persecuted for their depredations on smallstock, still held their own until fairly recently, but within the last two decades jackal-proof fences, traps, rifles, strychnine baits and cyanide cannons have reduced both species to a few remnant populations and wandering individuals.

Nowadays no wild animal symbolises the southern plains of Namibia more than the springbok. "Seldom will one ever behold a more beautiful picture in the animal world than a

fleeing herd of these graceful gazelles," wrote one early traveller in Namibia. "They begin to cut their strange capers; then set off at top speed, now and then giving long high leaps . . . Along their backs they have long white hairs, which are hidden by a fold of skin when the animal stands, but which, when they leap, is folded out most effectively into a waving mane."

To view springbok "pronking" across a broad open plain is indeed a memorable sight, especially in the early morning, when there is still a nip in the air and the strange compulsion to pronk seems particularly infectious. Frequently it is the younger animals that first start to bounce up and down on stiff straight legs, their snowy pennants raised into the chill breeze; but the fever quickly spreads, and soon wherever one looks the plains are alive with bucking and bobbing bodies that dance gaily between other more sedate species as if possessed by an uncontrollable zest for life.

The behaviour pattern of springbok pronking acts as a group signal warning others in the vicinity of the presence of possible danger. Usually such bouts are initiated by the approach of a jackal, cheetah, motor vehicle or other potential predator. A springbok ewe will also pronk in front of her lamb in order to attract its attention and lead it out of danger. Pronking when excited is so instinctive in springbok that they sometimes continue even while being chased, which can seriously reduce the individual's chances of escape.

In the previous century springbok were widespread and apparently very abundant in the south of Namibia, and it is probable that they embarked periodically on mass migrations such as those recorded in the northern Cape at this time. Eye witness estimates of the animal numbers that took part in these remarkable treks range from one hundred thousand to many millions.

In 1850, the hunter Gordon Cumming "beheld the plains and even the hillsides, which stretched away on every side, thickly covered, not with herds, but with one living mass of springbok; as far as the eye could strain . . . giving a whitish tint to the veld as though there had been a light fall of snow."

The reasons for these enormous springbok migrations, which appear to have occurred irregularly in place and time, are still not fully understood, but they probably related to the cycles of high and low rainfall years that feature naturally in the arid zones of Southern Africa. After successive seasons of high rainfall, springbok numbers would have increased rapidly, but in the lean years that followed, the population would have been too high for available grazing and huge concentrations of animals would have congregated wherever showers of rain had produced a flush of new green grass. The forage in such areas would quickly have been grazed off and the springbok forced to move on, continually in search of fresh pastures. If none were available they might then have trekked blindly *en masse* across the veld until either the drought was relieved or else large numbers died of starvation — or thirst — leaving bleached bones scattered across this vast and virtually uninhabited region.

With the introduction of sheep into southern Namibia the springbok population declined rapidly and probably reached an all-time low of less than 50 000 around the middle of this century. However, the eradication of the springboks' natural enemies such as jackal and caracal, coupled with an increasing awareness among farmers that these beautiful animals are a marketable resource, has led to a steady rise in their numbers during recent years. Today it is estimated that there are probably more than 200 000 springbok in the region.

The rock hyrax or dassie is another species that has benefited by man's eradication of its natural predators. Although always plentiful on the hills and rocky koppies in the south, the numbers of these little animals were previously kept in check by leopard, caracal and the larger birds of prey; whilst a healthy jackal population ensured that they did not venture too far from hillsides where they could scuttle quickly into rock crevices whenever danger threatened. Dassies are indeed voracious feeders, and where they occur in large numbers their browsing can have a considerable adverse effect on the vegetation.

Dassies are not the only animals that periodically reach plague proportions in southern Namibia. Since prehistoric times immense numbers of locusts have hatched in years when weather conditions were favourable. Young locusts have no wings and move around in a localized area by walking or hopping, and are thus known as *voetgangers* in Afrikaans. It is only as adults that they develop wings enabling them to form the great swarms that may migrate for many hundreds of kilometres across the country, causing enormous damage to crops and grazing wherever they settle.

A more insidious plague over extensive tracts in the south is caused by harvester termites, which carry off large quantities of dry grass for storage in their underground nests. In healthy veld with good grass cover the amount of dry material they remove is normally insignificant, but in overgrazed veld their effect can be considerable, and many a farmer has set aside a camp for later grazing only to find that when it is needed much of the standing grass crop has already been transported underground by these hard-working little insects.

Two tireless predators, the aardwolf and the bat-eared fox, help to control harvester termites. Unfortunately, on some farms the indiscriminate use of poison and traps has reduced the numbers of these animals, which has in turn enabled termite populations to explode, often causing the farmer a greater 'hidden' economic loss than the sheep predators he had attempted to destroy.

Guinea fowl and francolin are also capable of eating prodigious numbers of termites, both while the insects are out harvesting and during their nuptial flights; and on farms where these birds are abundant the population of harvester termites is maintained within safe levels. However, both guinea fowl and francolin require ground cover for breeding, so that once again it is the condition of the veld that is the critical factor in controlling these pests.

Plagues of dassies, termites and locusts have all added to the hardships of the few steadfast men and women who have made the arid south of Namibia their home. Here in this harsh and unforgiving region even the good years are droughts by normal standards. In spite of this, the scorched plains and stark mountains have a strange fascination that exerts an inexplicable hold over its sunburned inhabitants, and the adversity that is part of everyday life has engendered a fierce pride in their hard-won achievements.

Previous page:
The Orange River, forming
Namibia's southern border,
meanders slowly
through a broad valley
carved between the Richtersveld
and the Hunsberge.

Left: Still relatively inaccessible and
virtually unexplored, the Hunsberge are the least
known of Namibia's mountain ranges.

Right: Associated with rocky outcrops and mountain slopes,
the Kokerboom or Quiver Tree *(Aloe dichotoma)* is a typical plant of the
south. The name derives from the Bushman custom of prising out the fibrous pith
inside the branches to make quivers for their poisoned arrows.

Below: Vervet monkeys *(Cercophithecus aethiops)* are common along the
riverine woodland that fringes the Orange River. Mainly tree-dwellers, these diurnal primates are
gregarious in habit, often forming small troops or family parties. By jumping from tree
to tree they can travel at great speed, and at night they roost in large trees.
Their diet consists of fruit, seeds, insects, and birds' eggs and nestlings. The single offspring
is carried on the underside of the mother's body for the first few months after birth.

The chameleon *Chamaeleo namaquensis*
is adapted to a harsh dry habitat.

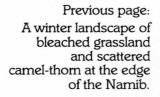

Previous page:
A winter landscape of
bleached grassland
and scattered
camel-thorn at the edge
of the Namib.

Right: Now only a series of deep still pools,
the Fish River winds tortuously between spectacular
quartzite cliffs towards its confluence
with the Orange.

Above: Communal domicile for perhaps
200 birds, the nest of the sociable weaver is a
masterpiece of co-operative construction.

Left: From across the Naute Dam, the Klein Karasberge
catch the last rays of sunlight.

Overleaf: Reflection from a setting sun.

A white-faced owl,
common nocturnal raptor of the savanna.

Left: Granite outcrop in the Grünau district.

Overleaf: The *Mukarob* ('Finger of God'),
an eroded remnant of a disintergrating
plateau in the arid south.

Above: *Hoodia gordonii*, a spiky succulent that is
cross-pollinated by flies which are attracted to its large flowers
by the strong odour of putrid meat they exude.

Opposite: (left) Chanting goshawks
are the most widespread birds of prey in Namibia.

Previous page:
Top left: Tufts of Bushman grasses sparsely
cover a low dune in the far south.

Bottom left: A meerkat family
at the entrance to its burrow in the
south-western Kalahari.

Right: Typical resident
of the bushveld, a white-backed vulture
perches on the branch of an acacia.

When good rains fall in the south a rich profusion of
wild flowers brings colour to the veld.

Above: *Asthenatherum glaucum*, one of the most palatable grasses of the
Kalahari region, is an important food source for gemsbok.

Opposite page:
Left, above: *Didelta spinosa*
Left, below: *Momordica humilis*
Right, above: *Cucumis africana*
Right, below: *Sisyndite spartea*

Previous page: Even a year after good rains, the exposed veld in the pre-Namib is covered with dry but nutritious grasses (*Stipagrostis ciliata*).

Right: Sunset over Hardap Dam.

Namib:
The great
coastal desert

Early on a cold, grey and foggy morning, a small black beetle emerges from beneath the sand and plods deliberately up the steep, wind-rippled incline of a large dune. Periodically it pauses, apparently summoning strength into the stiff joints of its hard thin legs, before once more resuming its slow progress up the slope. Finally at the summit the beetle faces into a soft swirling breeze and then gradually straightens its rear legs and lowers its head as if in supplication to some misty deity. As the soft moisture-laden clouds drift across the dunes, the beetle remains motionless in its strange stance. After a while tiny droplets of water condense on its smooth shiny back where they trickle downwards, coalescing into a single bubble of water that hangs from its mouth. The beetle drinks in this water.

On a nearby dune another smaller and rounder beetle bulldozes its way through the soft sand industriously excavating a thin trench at right angles to the fog-bearing wind. The two slight parallel ridges along the trench's rim also precipitate water from the damp air and, as the beetle crawls back along its path, it sucks up the moisture that has collected between the sand grains.

When they have drunk their fill the two beetles dig their way back under the loose surface sand leaving only their tracks as evidence of their passing. These little tenebrionids *Onymacris unguicularis* and *Lepidochora discoidalis,* have just demonstrated two of the most extraordinary behavioural adaptations in the animal kingdom. Both beetles are relatively common inhabitants of the dune Namib, a vast sea of restless sand that has been sculpted by ceaseless winds into the largest shifting dunes on Earth. Many other fascinating creatures inhabit these dunes: legless lizards, delicate web-footed geckos with translucent skins, weird dancing spiders, side-winding adders that ambush their prey by burying all but their heads in the sand and, perhaps strangest of all, the Namib

golden mole — a voracious predator that 'swims' blindly through the loose sand, finding its prey by their vibrations. These species are all primarily nocturnal — night-shift workers that emerge only at dusk and disappear before dawn into the cool depths beneath the sand — but during the day other equally fascinating creatures are abroad, all perfectly adapted to their harsh, waterless habitat.

The Namib is however not all dunes. There are also bleak gravel plains, stark rock inselbergs, treacherous salt pans, awesome gorges and forbidding mountain ranges. Near the coast on the barren gravel wastelands where no blade of grass, no twig of brush, relieves the enormous desolation, the desert can arouse feelings of apprehension, even fear, but then the sun's evening rays on distant smoky-blue mountains viewed across quiet tree-speckled plains can create a mood of deep tranquillity.

The Namib is the oldest of the world's deserts — a strange and complex region that has no equal on Earth. Superficially it can be described as a long coastal desert that stretches from the Olifant's River in South Africa, up along the length of Namibia, over the sunbaked plains to north of Moçamedes in Angola. At its widest it is nearly 150 kilometres across, but its eastern edge is often difficult to define, depending much on the structure of the landscape, the benevolence of the seasons and the activities of man.

Climatically, the Namib is regarded as a cool desert although the inland zone can often experience blistering hot days, and even the coastal belt is periodically scorched by fierce east winds that have been heated over the sunbaked plains of the interior. It is one of the many anomalies of the desert that these east winds frequently blow in winter so that the hottest days of the year may be recorded during June and July.

Namibia's coast is one of the driest places on Earth. Here in this desolate region, the revered statistics of our technological society are found wanting. To quote average rainfall at a particular point as 12 mm per year, when, in fact, the total amount recorded has fallen as one or two heavy downpours per decade, is indeed misleading. Even in the inland regions where annual averages range from 50 to 100 mm, it is not unusual for two years' rain to fall in the space of a fortnight.

If there is one common denominator in all the varied landscapes of the Namib then it is the *Soo-oop-wa*, the cold south-westerly wind that seems to blow incessantly off the icy South Atlantic Ocean, cooling the land and modelling the desert sands into the great dunes that characterise some of the Namib's most striking scenery.

The *Soop-oop-wa*, however, does not always blow; perhaps for one day in every five the wind alters direction to a more moderate north-westerly.

In the chill of the evening, the water vapour carried by this changed wind condenses into thick banks of fog that creep stealthily over the desert during the night, shrouding the Namib in life-giving mist.

East winds also periodically blow fierce and hot, rousing the surface sands and withering the desert plants. The east winds bring no moisture, but, to the driest parts of the desert, they carry an equally valuable burden — food, in the form of plant and animal detritus from the better-watered interior, and seeds for future generations of hardy grasses and xerophytic annuals.

The story of the Namib really begins along the coast - on the long windswept beaches that have few significant rocky outcrops and only sparse scrubby halophytic vegetation.

The aspect of the Namibian coastline is in fact so bleak and desolate that it is a surprise to find any life here at all; and yet on these barren shores there are the largest mainland fur seal colonies in the world as well as literally millions of sea birds that feed, rest and in some cases breed along the coast.

Clearly, these inhospitable beaches could not in themselves sustain such an abundance of life and, as study is made tracing the various food chains — continually seeking the prey of the preyed upon — it becomes clear that almost all coastal creatures depend ultimately on a single remarkable resource: microscopic, free-floating marine plants which occur in immense numbers in the cold waters of the Benguela Current. These planktonic plants depend in turn on periodic upwellings of deep sea water that is especially rich in nitrate and phosphate salts. When this highly fertile water rises to the surface near the Namibian coast it provides an ideal medium for plant growth, thus forming the foundation of an exceptionally diverse and productive ecosystem that in terms of biomass has few equals anywhere.

Similar upwellings of nutrient-rich water occur along the Peruvian and Californian coasts, and in these areas, as on the coast of Southern Africa, they support enormous shoals of filter-feeding fish. Unfortunately, man's lack of foresight has led to over-exploitation and the consequent collapse or decline of fishing and processing industries that were established to harvest the shoals — a resource that once seemed inexhaustible.

When the numbers of shoal fish off Namibia's coast declined man was not the only predator to be affected. Numerous larger fish as well as cormorants, pelicans, gannets, penguins and many other birds also thrived on these great shoals of pilchards and anchovies, and inevitably their populations were adversely affected.

Cape fur seals that live along the Namib coast feed on a variety of marine organisms including crab, squid, rock lobster and considerable quantities of fish. They have been known to follow in the wake of the little seine trawlers, exploiting the boats' highly sophisticated sonar equipment in order to locate the shoals. This habit has not endeared the seals to fishermen, especially when, as the boat nears a shoal, they spurt ahead in a feeding spree, dispersing the fish before the nets can be deployed.

Every year in October massive bull seals, each weighing up to 300 kilograms, haul their bloated bodies up onto the beaches to stake territorial claims to a few square metres of bare rock or barren sand. From the moment the seals arrive, these insignificant plots on an endless shore are fiercely contested and savagely fought over, for it is only by holding a territory in the chosen breeding area that a bull becomes eligible to gather around him a harem of the sleek, lissom cow seals which arrive in order to give birth to single pups a few weeks later.

Within a week of giving birth, the female fur seal comes into oestrus again and she will be mated by the bull in whose territory she has pupped. Remarkably, the pregnancy does not begin immediately, for a seal's gestation period is only eight months, and in order to enable her to pup again exactly a year later, the fertilized ovum is held in the cow's fallopian tubes for nearly four months before it moves on to the uterus where implantation occurs and cell division begins.

Once a bull seal has established a territory he dare not vacate it for more than a few minutes and must consequently spend almost the entire breeding season on land, relying on the heavy layers of blubber he has built up to sustain him. By the time the last cow has conceived some bulls may have lost over 100 kilograms in weight, but their role in the maintenance of the species is then at an end and they can now range the open seas, only occasionally returning to the breeding area until finally, the following October, an overriding sexual drive directs their wanderings back to the disputed beaches.

Soon after mating, cow seals return to the sea to feed, sometimes leaving their offspring for many days on end. During their mothers' absence the pups congregate in huge nurseries. A cow probably finds her own pup when she returns to the beach by sound, but to anyone who has seen or heard the bedlam of a seal colony with small pups, her apparently unerring ability to locate her own progeny is truly remarkable.

It is imperative for the seals to breed in such vast colonies and all virtually within a few weeks of one another. Synchronised breeding reduces the period that the bulls must spend on the beaches; but there is another important advantage in this behaviour. Were the cows to give birth throughout the year in smaller groups, the pups, which are slow-moving and helpless when young, would provide a year-round source of food for a resident predator population that would annually account for a high percentage of the pup crop. As it is, many jackals do gather around the colonies' periphery during the short breeding season, but the number of pups is so enormous that their toll has little overall effect.

In recent times, however, the fur seals' evolutionary response to its natural enemies has, in fact, made it more vulnerable to a new species of predator that prizes not the pups' flesh but their smooth densely-haired pelts. For over 300 years now, man has commercially cropped the young fur seals along Namibia's coast, and in the past many of the more accessible colonies were ruthlessly decimated. Today all sealing operations in Southern Africa are strictly controlled, and in spite of an annual harvest of 70 000 pups there are well over half a million seals breeding between Cape Cross and the Orange River and their numbers are, in fact, increasing.

The inland Namib is dissected by a number of seasonal rivers that descend from the interior plateau and meander across the arid landscape. The banks of the larger watercourses are ringed with stately trees that testify to the fact that water does flow underground even if not on the surface. The desert rivers play a vital role in the ecology of the region for they provide shade, forage and a supply of protein-rich seed pods in areas where there is little other food or shelter available. They also bring a touch of green to the otherwise sere desert scenery.

The Kuiseb, down which Alexander pioneered the first wagon route to the coast, is one of the larger seasonal rivers traversing the central Namib. Along its winding course there are dense woodlands of tall heavy-boled acacias, and in times of drought large numbers of game congregate in its bed in order to browse on fresh growth and compete with one another for the falling pods. The Kuiseb, however, brings more than just food and verdant colour to the desert, for its course also marks a truly dramatic change in the face of the Namib.

To the south of this river lies a vast sea of sand that has been moulded by the wind into long lines of massive dunes extending all the way to Lüderitzbucht, over 500 kilometres down the coast. At its widest point the sand sea is over 100 kilometres across, making it the largest continuous dune field in the world. Along the southern bank of the Kuiseb, massive red dunes tower menacingly above the riverbed, dwarfing the riverine trees and providing vistas of spectacular contrast. The menace of the dunes is real, for during the dry season they encroach into the river bed, sending long fingers of windblown sand across the cracked, dry mud. During dry climatic cycles, whole trees may be enveloped and smothered by the moving sands, but then suddenly, often without any warning to the scattered residents along the Kuiseb's lower course , a chocolate-coloured wall of water — runoff from violent storms deep inland — thunders down the riverbed and, within a matter of hours, sweeps away all gains the dunes have made.

Excepting near the coast, where the relentless northwards creep of the sands has breached the riverbed, this dynamic balance between the Kuiseb's floodwaters and the shifting dunes has kept the north bank of the river free of sand. Here the Namib surface is naked with desolate gravel plains stretching endlessly to grey, virtually featureless horizons; and only occasional dark ridges of dolerite or low outcrops of shattered granite relieve the overwhelming monotony of the landscape.

Shallow drainage lines are marked by brittle branched shrubs or a sparse stubble of withered grey grass; but apart from this, the gravel plains are barren and apparently lifeless. However, just below the soil surface there are tiny plant seeds patiently awaiting the magical touch of a once-in-a-decade shower of rain. For some Namib plants just a single hard downpour measuring less than 15 mm can provide sufficient moisture for them to germinate, grow to maturity and set seed, all in the space of two weeks. When this occurs the desert blooms, albeit only for a transient moment.

Within days, a pale green shimmer will appear on the plains as countless little grass seedlings sprout and stretch their new leaves in the sunlight. A fortnight later the tufts are fully grown, and as they wave gently in the breeze they release vast numbers of silver, featherlight seeds, that are wafted upwards to drift for kilometres across the plains.

The seed of the desert Bushman grass is one of nature's miracles of micro-engineering, for not only is the tiny seed head attached to a long feathery awn designed to catch the wind and lift the seed into the air, but when it finally lands, two delicate auxiliary awns form a tripod with the seed head, ensuring that its spiral point is in contact with the ground. In the ensuing days the feathered awn is wafted to and fro by the breeze, gradually boring the seed up to half a centimetre into the ground. Here it will lie, safe from seed-eating creatures, until sufficient rain falls to activate it and initiate another ephemeral life cycle.

The plants of the true deserts, where long drought separates the brief periods when sufficient moisture is available for growth, can broadly be grouped into two categories: the drought-evaders and the drought-survivors. The drought-evaders include the annual grasses, and many other short-lived plants, that die off when the soil dries out, relying on their dormant seeds to maintain the species until the next rain. The drought-survivors, on the other hand, have evolved a variety of tactics that enable them to withstand soil dehydration.

Succulents store moisture in their swollen stems or leaves, whilst other drought-survivors store water in large underground rhizomes. Some of the larger plants have exceptionally long roots that reach deep underground and tap the soil water table where a continuous supply of water is available even during droughts. The tap roots of the camel-thorn, *Acacia erioloba*, have been known to penetrate over 15 metres into the ground, and it is this adaptation that allows the species to grow into a sizeable tree where few other plants survive.

Perhaps the most remarkable drought-surviving technique, however, is the ability to withstand extreme tissue desiccation — in some cases, to a cell fluid content of less than 5%. Here the amazing *Myrothamnus flabellifolius,* or 'resurrection plant' as it is commonly called, immediately comes to mind. This little shrub, plentiful on the slopes of many inland ranges in the central and northern Namib, has acquired its common name through the ability of a dry, apparently dead stem to sprout green leaves within a couple of hours of being placed in a jar

of water. In their natural habitat, a drab grey hillslope of dormant resurrection plants will turn bright green overnight after just a light shower.

When rain falls in the Namib, the gravel plains explode into exuberant life. Insects emerge from aestivation or hatch out of long-buried eggs, while numerous birds and many larger animals migrate from the interior in order to exploit the temporary abundance. For the true Namib however, such occasions are infrequent and brief: soon the scorching sun and dry desert winds will suck the moisture from the gravel once more, withering the plants and forcing the game to move back inland.

Unable to migrate, the smaller desert creatures must seek sanctuary below the earth or perish, adding their bodies to the wind-blown detritus which will sustain the few that survive the drought. However, although many do die, enough of each species always survive, as eggs or aestivating adults, to repopulate the plains when rain once more coaxes the desert plains back into life.

From the Kuiseb, the gravel flats extend virtually uninterrupted to just south of the Ugab River, where the first crumpled ranges of the 'Skeleton Coast' sprawl across the plains, introducing the rugged mountain scenery of the legendary Kaokoveld.

The inland Namib, often referred to as the pro- or pre-Namib, is perhaps the most attractive part of this region. Here the desert reveals its most benign face, for rainfall is more regular and in most years the plains support a sward of hardy perennial grasses. Projecting through the superficial sand or gravel floor of the pro-Namib there are many inselberg outcrops, while along their upper reaches the larger seasonal rivers have incised deep gorges and grotesque moonscapes through the ancient rock formations.

When above-average quantities of rain fall in this part of the desert the plains are transformed into a vast wind-rippled sea of bright emerald that quickly matures to tawny yellow and shimmering silver as the wispy seedheads ripen. At such times most of the larger Namib animals feed almost exclusively on the succulent and protein-rich young grass shoots, deriving sufficient fluid from their food to make them independent of drinking water and thus able to range at will across the picturesque landscape. Once the grasses mature, however, the moisture content of their leaves steadily decreases from over 80% while still green, to less than 20% when the tuft is parched and dormant, forcing the desert animals to rely on various physiological and behavioural adaptations in order to maintain their body-fluid requirements.

In some respects, the pro-Namib is an even harsher environment than the coastal Namib for here, although the annual average rainfall is significantly greater, fog is much less frequent and day temperatures are considerably higher. Heat stress, which is seldom a factor near the coast, can become critical further inland, particularly during the long dry months before the first summer showers.

During the day the smaller Namib creatures, which gain heat quickly, must seek shelter under the earth or in the shade of a rock or small plant; but for the larger species, escape from the midday sun is often impossible. Gemsbok, one of the largest permanent residents of the Namib, may frequently be encountered standing quietly on completely barren plains when air temperatures rise well over 40°C.

Because normal body-cooling mechanisms such as sweating or panting entail a considerable water loss, the gemsbok cannot employ them, and in the brain-boiling sunshine, their body temperatures may rise to as high as 45°C. It has been found, however, that the temperature of blood circulating through the gemsbok's brain is considerably lower than the temperature of its body, a phenomenon explained by the presence of a tight knot of capillaries in the animal's sinus cavities, where arterial blood flowing to the brain is cooled both by water evaporation in the damp nasal cavities and also by heat exchange with venous blood returning from the brain.

Behaviour can also play a considerable role in reducing the build-up of body heat. If no shade is available, gemsbok will seek any promontory in order to exploit to the maximum the cooling effect of the slightest breeze.

Even the gemsbok's characteristic slow canter when disturbed is designed to minimise energy expenditure and heat generation. It is actually dangerous for a gemsbok to extend itself during hot weather, a fact that was quickly learned during early game capture operations when some of these animals died as a result of overheating and consequent brain damage.

Although gembsok can survive without water when green grass or edible succulents are available, during prolonged dry periods they develop water deficits that must be balanced by long treks to the few widely scattered waterholes. In times of drought they are capable of covering enormous distances in search of areas where light showers have coaxed a little green growth from the parched plains. In the past they often migrated deep inland at such times, but the fencing-off of sheep farms along the Namib's eastern border has cut off this traditional inland migration, and large concentrations of game along the farm boundaries has sometimes caused habitat degradation and high mortalities.

In order to relieve the situation, sub-economic farmland between the Namib Desert Park and the Naukluft has been purchased and further border farm acquisitions have been proposed in the Rosh Pinah area.

Scientifically only the first steps have been taken to unravel some of the Namib's wondrous secrets and strange enigmas. It is indeed a fragile region — vast, but very vulnerable to abuse — where a road can be obliterated in a single sand storm and yet a solitary vehicle can leave tracks that last a decade.

The sound conservation of the Namib is one of the greatest challenges facing the present generation, for this desert is unique, not only in Southern Africa, but in the world. Here are some of the strangest living plants and animals in a habitat that defies generalizations; a region that is fearsome, mysterious and breathtakingly beautiful.

Cape gannets, attracted by an abundance of pelagic fish,
breed in large colonies on scattered islands that lie off the desert coast.

Right: Gemsbok gallop across broad mudflats
near the mouth of the Orange River.

Previous pages:
The desolate shores of the southern Namib are
a hostile environment to man but a significant habitat for vast numbers
of seabirds and fur seals.

Almost perfectly in step, two pairs of cock ostriches
race across the slopes of a pale coastal dune.

Lashed by turbulent seas
and dangerous currents,
the *Sperrgebiet* desert coast has,
with good reason, retained
a fearsome reputation.
In the background,
Bogenfels Rock forms
a spectacular natural arch
60 metres high through which,
if the wild seas allowed,
a ship could easily pass.
Because of the abundance
of diamonds on this coast,
strict regulations
governing entry have
preserved the area as a
unique natural wilderness,
virtually unvisited by man.

Above: A rare visitor from the icy waters of the distant South Atlantic, a bull elephant seal emits a threatening roar.

Below: A Cape fur seal cow keeps watch over a nursery of two-month-old pups.

Above: Fur seals breed in large colonies
along the inhospitable desert coast.

Overleaf:
Left, above: Cow fur seals rest briefly on a bleak sandy shore.

Left, below: Outside of the short breeding season,
fur seal bulls are infrequent visitors to the coastal colonies.

Right: Scattered groups of fur seals, taking advantage
of a clear windless day, bask in the sunshine.

Above: *Mesembryanthemum crystallinum*,
a hardy succulent of the coastal sand plains,
shown here in its resting stage.

Below: *Mesembryanthemum cryptanthum*,
commonly known as 'boiled fingers'.

Left: Biological evidence suggests that the Namib
is the world's oldest desert.

Previous page:
Above: 'Dik Willem',
a prominent landmark in the
southern Namib, is a massive
inselberg visible from up to
50 km away in most directions.

Below: The curved
outlines of dunes near
Sossusvlei have been sculpted
by strong easterly winds.
The highest shifting
sand dunes in the world
(350 metres or more),
their reddish hue is due to the
presence of iron oxide
covering the grains of sand.

Right: Dwarfed by
a towering sand dune,
two large camel-thorns
(Acacia erioloba) obtain
life-giving moisture by
tapping the subterranean
flow of the Tsauchab River.
The longest of a number
of westward-flowing
periodical rivers arising
from springs in the
Naukluft Mountains,
the Tsauchab ends in
Sossusvlei in a valley
among the sand dunes.

Right: Above: A female plant of *Welwitschia mirabilis*, a primitive gymnosperm that occurs only in the Namib. The plant has two leaves which continue to grow throughout its lifespan, believed to exceed 1 000 years.

Below, left: A burrowing adder *(Bitis peringueyi)* ambushes its prey of small lizards and geckos by burying its body beneath the loose sand.

Below, right: Two tenebrionid beetles *(Onymacris bicolor)* conserve moisture by moving along the desert dunes riding one upon the other.

Below: Although apparently lifeless, the Namib supports a unique ecosystem of desert-adapted plants and animals.

Left: In the 'Moon Valley', tributaries
of the Swakop River, that might flow but once in ten years,
have over countless ages created
a strange lunar-like landscape.

Following page: Deep folds
incised in the landscape in the vicinity of
the Kuiseb Canyon, which cuts a
deep rift in the escarpment of the Khomas Hochland
just on the boundary of the Namib Desert Park.

After heavy rainfall the normally barren gravel plains of
the Namib are transformed to soft shades of green.

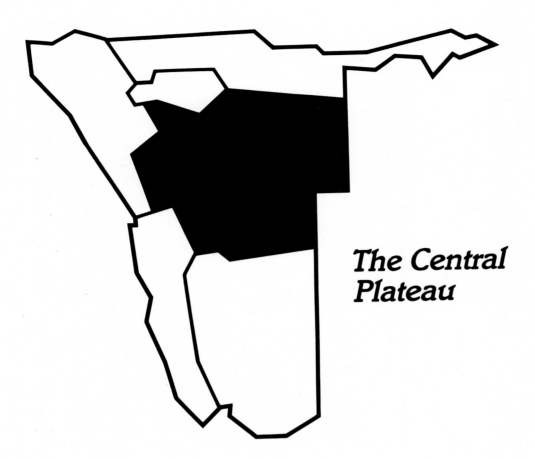

The Central Plateau

"An hour might have elapsed when I observed in a distant glen a dark object . . . we proceeded towards the spot and I soon saw that the shapeless mass was nothing less than a rhinoceros. With now noiseless and quickened step and our guns on full cock, we made up to the monster, which still gave no signs of life. At last, however, one of us whistled; on which, and with the rapidity of thought, the beast sat up on its haunches and surveyed us with a curious and sulky look. But it was only a moment; for, before he had time to get on his legs, two well directed balls laid him prostrate within half a dozen paces of our feet."

So wrote Namibia's most famous hunter-explorer, Charles John Andersson, describing his first rhinoceros hunt, having been in the country only a few days. Andersson went on to shoot "upwards of one hundred" rhino during his wanderings in South Western Africa between 1850 and 1867.

Such was life in this part of Africa during the middle of the nineteenth century where every new immigrant, be he trader, explorer or missionary, carried a gun with which he blazed away for sport, profit or simply to provide the daily ration. Francis Galton, another early explorer in Namibia, wrote:

"I like rhinoceros flesh more than any other wild animal. A young calf rolled up in a piece of spare hide and baked in the earth is excellent. I hardly know which of the little animal is best, the skin or the flesh."

Of course it could not last; for Namibia is predominantly an arid land and consequently, although at one time big game was widespread in the interior, it was never more than locally abundant. By the end of the century rhino and elephant had been driven into the far north of the country. In 1897 the rinderpest epidemic that had already scourged east and south Africa, struck Namibia, wiping out the buffalo herds and decimating many other species as well as domestic livestock. For wildebeeste, hartebeeste and the larger predators, the death knell was, however, sounded by the arrival of white farmers.

But not all the big game was exterminated. Some species have actually increased as a result of vegetation changes and new artificial waters created by Namibia's farmers for their stock. Furthermore, as a result of some of the most advanced conservation legislation in Africa, game farming and trophy hunting have recently become lucrative propositions for land owners, which has encouraged the conservation of certain species. National parks and game reserves have also been established, some of which now rank with the finest in the continent. Slowly the game is coming back to Namibia's interior. There are still problems to be faced and legislation to be further improved, but the overall trends in game conservation are healthy.

The central plateau of Namibia extends northwards from the broken highlands around Windhoek and Rehoboth, and east of the great escarpment that towers above the coastal plain. In the Khomas Hochland the plateau is characterised by deeply incised watercourses and rugged rolling hills, many of which reach elevations in excess of 2 000 metres. Soon, however, the landscape flattens out into broad level plains that stretch to a faded blue horizon.

On the main road between Okahandja and Otavi, nearly 300 kilometres to the north of Windhoek, the skyline is broken only by the twin pyramid-like peaks of the Omatako mountains, a few stark ridges and the long table-topped sandstone massif of the Waterberg. East of the Waterberg is the 'Omaheke', a perfectly flat sand plain that extends uninterrupted to the Botswana border, 400 kilometres distant.

At the north-western periphery of the plateau the dramatic Brandberg massif looks out over great desert plains that

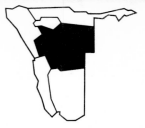

extend towards the forbidding Skeleton Coast. At 2 568 metres, it is the highest mountain in Namibia. In ages past this vast mass of granite was thrust upwards by incomprehensible forces initiated during a major faulting of the earth's crust. Exposed to the elements, the steep slopes were subsequently carved and weathered by the wind and infrequent rain into the rugged features that can be seen today.

The Spitzkoppe, 90 kilometres south of the Brandberg, form another striking landmark between plateau and desert. The Groot Spitzkop itself, a stark granite monolith rising 600 metres above the parched gravel, is one of the finest inselbergs in existence; while just to the east of it lies the equally spectacular dragon-backed Pontok mountain. Hunched over the adjoining plains are many other bare granite hills — all dwarfed by the Spitzkop and Pontok, but each in its own right an impressive rock formation.

At the base of the Spitzkop there is a large rock overhang adorned with delicate Bushman paintings that include antelope, giraffe, an exceptionally beautiful mountain zebra, a large black rhino, and a majestic maned lion. There are also numerous highly animated human figures. Here, in this magnificent valley of granite, the Bushmen, Africa's ancient artists, must have lived an idyllic life; for water is plentiful in the deep rock pools that collect after rain showers and, judging from their paintings, game must also have been abundant.

Travelling northwards from Windhoek there is increasing evidence of a higher annual rainfall. The trees become noticeably taller and more closely spaced, and even the hills have a softer outline and appear less gaunt, their steep slopes covered with a thin veneer of coarse gritty soil that cloaks their rocky skeletons and supports a scrubby smattering of bush. For a few months each summer this region can appear quite lush as the season's new growth carpets the plains and tints the ranges with subtle hues of green. The impression is fleeting, however, for the autumn sun quickly cures the grasses and bleaches the landscape to pale yellow and dusty shades of grey.

The vegetation of the high plateau consists mainly of thorny savanna dominated by various species of acacia: *Acacia karroo, A. tortilis, A. mellifera, A. erubescens, A. fleckii, A. hereroensis* are some of the most conspicuous. In spring and early summer, prior to the rainy season, these acacias are bedecked in masses of yellow, cream or white pompom blossoms that bring soft colour to the otherwise drab, monotonous scenery. Acacias are the picture-book trees of 'big game Africa'; a genus that characterises this continent like the pine in North America or the eucalyptus in Australia. There are twenty two species of acacia represented in Namibia and one or more members of this genus can be found in every terrestial habitat in the country excepting the almost barren coastal strip. Acacias are most at home in arid regions where their feathery, twice compound leaves, composed of many tiny leaflets, decrease the leaf surface area, thus reducing water loss by transpiration. All species of this genus have protein-rich seed pods that are sought after by game and domestic animals with equal vigour. Moreover, being members of the legume family, their nitrate-producing roots play an important role in fertilizing the soil.

When the first farmers settled on the central plateau they found a region composed of broad grassy parklands with scattered trees. Scrub and bushes were confined to hillslopes and the vicinities of permanent springs, vleis and pans. In this habitat the introduced cattle thrived and all wild species that threatened or competed with a farmer's livestock were ruthlessly persecuted. Lion, wild dog and hyena were soon exterminated in all but the far north and east; while buffalo, wildebeeste and hartebeeste, which could carry contagious diseases transmittable to cattle, were shot at every opportunity. Fences, competition for water, and hunting for sport or food, all contributed to the demise of other wildlife populations, and by the second half of this century much of the central plateau sustained only monospecific ranching with exotic breeds of cattle. The first seeds of disaster had been sown.

In the past, apart from predators and disease, the general lack of permanent surface water had limited the numbers of wild game and the Herero and Nama cattle herds. Vast tracts of the region were naturally waterless throughout most of the year, and could thus only be grazed on a seasonal basis when summer thunderstorms filled the pans and brought the larger rivers down in temporary flood, leaving slowly receding pools along their courses. While this water was available, wildlife and native cattle exploited the grazing in these areas, but as the seasonal water dried up they were forced to return to the vicinity of permanent springs. Here, in their absence, the grasses had had a chance to regenerate after the previous dry season's grazing. Through the ages, Namibia's northern savannas had adapted to this natural system of rotational grazing, and although the numbers of animals they supported were relatively low, the grasses on the plains remained healthy and vigorous.

Where game and cattle had been unable to graze down the wet season's growth, the rank grasses would have stood parched and tinder dry throughout the frosty highland winter until they were ignited by spring lightning, a Bushman hunter or by the pastoralists themselves in their effort to rejuvenate the smothered grass tufts and provide a green flush with the coming of the first rains. In the central plateau there are few natural barriers to veld fire and consequently once ignited, the veld would have burned for weeks on end before heavy rain or a reverse in wind direction finally extinguished the flames. Until well into the 20th century fierce veld fires swept many parts of the highland plains annually, causing great damage to saplings and low bushes, thereby playing a major role in maintaining the open nature of the savanna. Only those areas where the grasses were naturally short and sparse, such as on rocky hillslopes, or where animal grazing had cropped down the swards, would have escaped this severe fire regime enabling plant succession to develop towards its climatic climax of dense woodland.

Subsequent to the Herero and Nama revolts at the turn of the century, white immigrants steadily settled much of the central pleateau where modern ranching practices were introduced in place of the more random grazing patterns of the wild game and herds of native livestock. At first the natural ecology of the region was little disturbed, but with their more advanced technology the new land-owners were soon able to eradicate predators effectively, reduce mortality from endemic stock diseases and, by the creation of artificial waters, open up vast tracts of previously waterless savanna to dry-season grazing. The settlers also brought with them fixed attitudes towards veld burning which was seen as an enormous waste of potentially valuable dry fodder. Legislation was therefore passed to outlaw deliberate setting alight of the veld, and all fires that started by accident or by natural causes were extinguished as a matter of urgency. A rapidly expanding network of roads and graded firebreaks also served to decrease the area subjected to veld fire.

Today, much of the highland plains is covered with dense thorny thickets that have crowded out the 'sweet' grasses and considerably reduced the livestock-carrying capacity of the region. In all too many cases this bush encroachment has led to overgrazing of the remaining open veld, which has in turn resulted in the destruction of perennial grasses and their replacement with less productive annuals. Without a perennial grass cover, the top-soil has been totally exposed to the elements, thereby reducing rain-water infiltration and accelerating the rate of erosion. The consequent drying out of the upper soil layers has further made it difficult to re-establish a perennial grass cover, which is the key to veld recovery and without which a sound fire regime is impossible. Since alternative methods of bush clearance are generally too costly, many cattle farmers are now locked into an apparently irreversible degradation cycle. In less than 100 years vast tracts of once highly productive pastures have been reduced to a dense tangled mass of thorny bushes — monuments to man's disregard for ecological principles and inability to farm in harmony with nature.

To the cattle rancher, who depends for his livelihood on a single grass-eating animal, the change in vegetation from open savanna to dense bush and thicket has been an unmitigated disaster; but in the natural order, the aspect of change is far from unusual, and the result has simply been a reshuffle of animal populations inhabiting the area. Where grazing species once predominated, browsers now thrive, and those species that have not been able to adapt to the new conditions have either emigrated or perished.

The wood-consuming termite, *Macrotermes michaelseni*, is one species that has been favoured by such changes in vegetation. Their large conical mounds, up to 3 metres in height, feature conspicuously throughout the central plateau plains. These giant mounds show considerable innovation in architectural design, ranging from tall thin spires to sturdy columns with blunt domes; there are even some twin tower residences with a choice of equal or unequal sized pinnacles. What determines the shape of the mound is still a mystery. It cannot be the 'king' or 'queen' since, after their nuptial flight, they remain in the egg-laying chamber deep inside the nest, never to see daylight again. And yet, apart from the royal pair, all other members of the colony, be they workers or soldiers, are of equal rank. Another puzzling aspect of termite mound construction is that nearly all the spires tilt slightly northwards.

Among the larger game animals, the kudu is probably the classic example of a species actually increasing in number as a result of modern man's manipulation of the habitat. Kudu are water-dependent browsing antelope that in the past probably occurred throughout Namibia, excepting along the desert coast; but their population would have been limited by the availability of drinking water. However, with the sinking of numerous boreholes on the central plateau and the now abundant supply of nutritious browse and pods, the numbers of this species have increased dramatically, and today there are probably more kudu in the territory than at any other time in the past.

An adult kudu bull is a magnificent beast with long spiral horns, one of the most sought-after big game trophies. Prior to 1958, trophy hunting was not officially recognised in Namibia, and even after this time existing legislation did little to encourage it. By law all game belonged to the State and could be hunted only during a short season on permit. As a result poaching was rife, particularly along the country's lonely roads — the so-called 'long farm' — and it was largely condoned by the general public who often sympathised with the poacher should he happen to be apprehended.

In 1967 a radical new nature conservation ordinance was introduced which gave, "the owner or occupier of a farm full ownership of all game, other than specially protected game, while such game is lawfully upon such farm and while such farm is enclosed with a sufficient fence". It furthermore made provision for the farmer to lease his hunting rights to any competent person and also gave the right to a visitor from overseas to hunt for trophies throughout the year. Largely as a result of this legislation, trophy hunting has today become a lucrative business in parts of Namibia. Since game animals now have a 'price' on their heads, landowners frequently go to considerable lengths to assist the authorities in their fight against illegal hunting.

The first nature conservation regulations in Namibia were introduced in 1892, just eight years after the country had been proclaimed a protectorate under the German flag. In this early legislation, hunting was permitted throughout the year, but permission had first to be obtained from the Governor. The only restrictions were that cow elephants could not be shot, and a closed season was laid down for the hunting of ostrich — much in demand at the time for their feathers. Ten years later, the first areas closed for hunting were established and in 1907 Governor von Lindequist proclaimed four of these as Game Reserves Nos. 1, 2, 3 and 4 respectively. The rest of the Territory was divided into districts, each with a District 'Chief', who had authority to enforce hunting seasons of varying duration, for the different game species in his district each year.

A new game preservation ordinance was passed in 1926 by which certain game species were listed as protected, including both elephant and rhino; and all trade in ivory and rhino horn became illegal. In order to shoot any of the other big game animals at that time, it was necessary to obtain a hunting licence from the Secretary for S.W.A. which, upon payment of £20, entitled the licence holder to kill or capture not more than sixteen animals of any species excepting those on the protected list. He was also required, within one month, to "furnish a return in writing, showing the number and sex and variation of big game killed by him". However, as no game wardens or nature conservators had been appointed, enforcement of these laws was left in the hands of

the police. In a territory as vast and remote as Namibia, this effectively meant that there was little control and poaching continued unabated, particularly in the more remote outlying districts.

The first officer charged solely to deal with nature conservation matters was appointed in 1947 and stationed at Otjiwarongo from where he was responsible for Game Reserve No. 2, which included the present Etosha National Park. Eight years later the first biologist, Mr. B.J.G. de la Bat, was appointed at Okaukuejo, inside the Park. In 1963 Mr. de la Bat was appointed director of the rapidly expanding Division of Nature Conservation and Tourism, a post he held until the end of 1980.

During his 25 years of involvement with nature conservation in Namibia, Mr. de la Bat was responsible for promoting much progress and expansion. The period between 1962 and 1972 alone saw the proclamation of ten new conservation areas with a combined extent of over 18 000 square kilometres and further new areas have subsequently been proclaimed. Together with the Etosha National Park and the Namib Desert Park, that were established during the German colonial period, the two Diamond Areas (where entry is prohibited and all fauna and flora strictly protected) and over 300 privately owned nature reserves, a total of more than 130 000 square kilometres, representing approximately 26% of the country's land surface, now enjoys some form of conservation status. Equally significant is the fact that out of fifteen vegetation zones recognised in the Territory, twelve are presently protected in recognised game reserves.

Prior to 1980, the Division of Nature Conservation and Tourism had no jurisdiction in homeland territories which were situated in the north and east of the country. During the late sixties and early seventies, increasing hunting pressures in these areas caused great concern to conservationists, particularly as within the homelands there were a number of species that did not occur, or were only poorly represented, in existing game parks. The outcome of this concern was a series of capture and translocation operations.

From Kaokoland and western Damaraland over 100 black-faced impala, a rare sub-species found only in northern Namibia and south-western Angola, as well as more than fifty black rhinoceros were moved to Etosha National Park, where thriving populations of both species were soon established. Roan, sable and tsessebe, three large antelope species that were threatened in the Kavango and Caprivi, were captured there and translocated to the Waterberg Plateau Park in the central highlands.

In 1975, the Division of Nature Conservation furthermore acquired from Natal a small number of white rhinoceros, a species that formerly occurred throughout much of north-eastern Namibia, but which had been shot out by hunters during the latter half of the last century. These huge animals were also released on the Waterberg massif where they have settled down well and started to breed.

The Cape buffalo was the last of the big game animals to be re-introduced onto the central plateau . At the time of the early exploration of Namibia, buffalo were recorded as widespread in the territory but the species was decimated by the 1897 rinderpest epidemic and remaining animals were subsequently exterminated in all areas except the Caprivi Strip. Unfortunately the danger of introducing certain stock diseases, for which buffalo are latent carriers, prohibited their translocation from the Caprivi, and it was only in 1980 that ten buffalo were obtained from the disease-free herd in the Addo National Park in South Africa. Like other threatened species, buffalo were also released on the Waterberg.

Besides endangered species, a number of other game animals have always occurred on the Waterberg. These include large numbers of eland, gemsbok and kudu. Hartebeeste, wildebeeste and giraffe were recently re-introduced from other reserves, or from farms where they were a problem.

Although it was only established in 1972, the Waterberg Plateau Park has become one of the most important game reserves in Namibia today. Situated in the centre of the acacia-dominated central highlands, the table-flat summit of the mountain, fifty kilometres long and up to sixteen kilometres broad, nevertheless supports a quite different plant community that is actually more akin to the sandveld, woodlands and savanna of the Territory's north-east. This is primarily due to the deep sandy nature of the soil and the fact that the plateau, which rises over 400 metres above the surrounding countryside, seems to 'capture' rain clouds as they sweep across the dry plains and thus receives a significantly higher average annual rainfall. Impressive sandstone cliffs that fringe all but the north-east end of the plateau form a natural barrier to game movements. All these factors combine to make this relatively small park an ideal sanctuary for threatened species, particularly those that favour a more moist habitat.

Today, the Waterberg can literally be described as a modern Noah's Ark, for as the rarer species breed up and become more abundant, excess animals will be used to re-stock other areas where their species have been shot out. The innovative and successful policy today being implemented in this park is indeed of great significance in the broad context of conservation in Africa.

Previous page: The Pontok Mountains, huge bald domes of granite, form part of the great Spitskoppe complex.

Below: *Cyphostemma juttae,* a succulent vine, is a conspicuous plant of the western plateau.

Right: *Albizia anthelmintica* in the Erongo Mountains. The bark of this tree is reputed to have medicinal qualities.

As a result of heavy rains in the interior, the Omaruru River comes down
in full flood. For most of the year, seasonal rivers such as this
are nothing more than expanses of dry sand
with a flow of subterranean water which supports the hardy trees
whose roots can reach it. Rainfall in the river's catchment area
will cause it to come down, which may happen twice or thrice a year,
or perhaps not at all for several years.

Above: A female *Agama planiceps*.
The agamas are common
highland lizards whose
characteristic habit of
bobbing their heads up
and down, especially
when nervous or curious,
is responsible for their
Afrikaans name *koggelmannetjie*.
These brightly coloured
rock-dwellers share,
to a lesser extent,
the chameleon's ability
to change colour.

Left: Dung beetles perform
a useful function in the veld ecosystem
by breaking down large pats
of dung. Prior to burial, the female
lays a single egg in the dungball
which subsequently provides
sustenance for the growing larva.

Above: The remarkable contrast before and after
rain in the Khomas Hochland.

Right: The Brandberg,
a massive block mountain geologically distinct from both
the Central Plateau and the Namib desert.

Common veld butterflies, *Belenois aurota*, habitually feed on dung.

Left: A rock fig clings precariously to lichen-covered sandstone cliffs
that define the perimeter of the Waterberg plateau and form a natural barrier
to game movements. The plateau, which rises 400 metres above
the acacia-dominated central highlands, receives a significantly higher
average annual rainfall and supports a quite different plant community from
the surrounding countryside. These factors combine to make
the relatively small Waterberg Plateau Park an ideal sanctuary for
threatened species, such as the black-faced impala, roan, sable, tsessebe,
white rhinoceros and Cape buffalo.

Overleaf: *Rynchelytrum repens,*
a pioneer annual grass conspicuous on disturbed veld.

Left, above: *Cleome* species
Left, below: *Sida hoepfneri*

Right, above: *Hibiscus praeteritus*
Right, below: *Indigofera alternans*

Opposite: *Sesamum capense* in the Khomas Hochland.

A female scarlet-chested sunbird feeds on the nectar of *Aloe hereroensis*.

Right: Huge granite cliffs form the western edge of the Erongo escarpment.

Overleaf:
Left: The 'Vingerklip', a distinctive column of
eroded sedimentary rock 35 metres high.

Right: Broad lightly wooded plains on the north-western plateau.

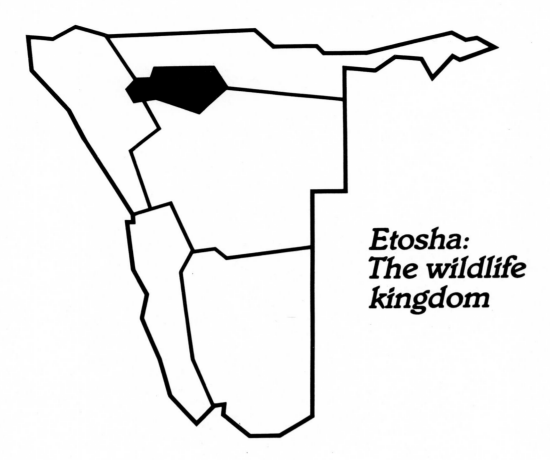

Etosha:
The wildlife
kingdom

On a broad treeless plain, six dapper zebra walk single file: in the lead, an old scarred mare, followed by two more adult mares, a foal and a yearling, while an immaculately striped stallion brings up the rear. It is a typical zebra family, and behind, other similar groups of five to eight stride purposefully in the same direction.

At the crest of a low rise, the first zebra group comes to a halt. Ahead lies the Etosha Pan — a vast shimmering expanse of salt-encrusted clay that stretches uninterrupted to the distant horizon. At the pan edge, less than sixty metres away, lies the objective of the morning's activity: a small stream of clear water that sparkles briefly in the sunlight before sinking below the pale Etosha mud. Now, so close to their destination, the zebras seem to have second thoughts. No other animals are drinking — a danger sign — but it is still early, and perhaps the other groups that stand restlessly watching the water have also only just reached the spring.

More zebras, a group of springbok and a small herd of wildebeeste arrive. The sun rises higher and the first heat waves start rippling off the pan. A few of the springbok move cautiously down to the water. They drink quickly and trot back to the safety of the ridge. The first zebras now edge closer, ears cocked and nostrils flared to catch the slightest scent of danger. More springbok drink, but the zebras are still cautious. They scrutinise every patch of sedge, every clump of grass before moving forward, a few steps at a time.

At the water a springbok suddenly shies: the zebras wheel around of one accord and gallop up the slope; but it is a false alarm and they soon turn and, after a good deal of nodding and barking, again approach the tantalising stream of cool water. Ten minutes later the lead mare is a few metres from the nearest pool. She stops and surveys the scene, then more confidently walks the last couple of steps to the water's edge.

Suddenly two lionesses explode out of a patch of sedge only metres from where the springbok had drunk.

Pandemonium reigns. The lead zebra turns in a flash and, showing a remarkable turn of speed, eludes both lionesses. The rest of the herd — a little further back — veer off to the side and gallop for safety. They seem to be well clear when, as if from nowhere, three more lionesses rise out of the dense grass directly in their path. Animals scatter in all directions and in their panic, two zebras collide and a yearling tumbles over in the swirling dust. Before it can rise, one of the lionesses is on top of it, a powerful paw across its face and fangs sunk deep into its throat. As the dust slowly settles the zebra kicks vainly for a few moments and then lies still.

After a short rest the lionesses drag their prey to the shade of a low acacia, where they are soon joined by two shaggy-maned lions and three cubs. With the lions still in full view, the plains game regroup and make their way cautiously back to the water where they quietly slake their thirst.

This is Etosha — the old Namibia, as it was before the White man, the Herero, Nama or even the Bushman came on the scene: a primordial kingdom ruled by tooth and claw, horn and tusk.

In order to understand the ecology of the Etosha National Park, it is important first to understand the Etosha Pan itself, for this sprawling saline desert, over 8 000 square kilometres in extent, exerts considerable influence on the rich and varied plant and animal life that has, since time immemorial, abounded on the adjoining plains.

During the Pleistocene age, some 100 000 years ago, Etosha was a lake, fed by permanently flowing rivers from the north; but as the great Kalahari depression filled with sand and the land dried out, the lake gradually became shallower. Later, as more sand was deposited and the land surface rose still further, the inflowing streams were diverted to the west and 'captured' by the river we now know as the Kunene. Without a permanent water supply the lake dried out; at first

only during dry cycles, but later more frequently, until today it is mostly dry, filling with water only briefly during years of above average rainfall. This intermittent flooding and drying out has caused the salts, carried in solution into the lake during past millennia, to become concentrated, thereby creating the pan's present highly saline surface.

Only three major channels — the Ekuma, Oshingambo and Omuramba Ovambo — now still regularly carry flood waters to the pan; but other smaller streams also flow into it during years of exceptional rainfall. The waters that flow down these waterways are by no means pure: apart from varying concentrations of soluble salts, they also carry silt, ranging from tiny particles of clay — so small that they are individually invisible to the naked eye — to relatively coarse sand. When they reach the pan, the flood waters fan out and lose velocity, adding their load of silt to the bottom mud. Later in the year when the pan once again dries out, much of this silt is blown off and deposited on the adjacent plains.

Because it is highly saline, periodically inundated, and at other times searing hot and desiccated, the actual pan surface is too harsh a habitat to support any perennial plant cover. However, as flood waters recede, salt-tolerant annual grasses germinate and quickly grow to maturity, exploiting the moist substrate that briefly prevails.

Just above the high flood level, both on the mainland and on raised islands in the pan itself, the first perennial plants become established. The most characteristic of these hardy pioneers is *Suaeda articulata*, a bushy halophyte with small succulent leaves. After rain, *Suaeda's* foliage turns dark green, but as the soil dries out, it changes to shades of orange or even wine red, providing a colourful border to the pan's sere surface.

The grasses *Sporobolus spicatus* and *Odyssea paucinervis* are other typical perennials of the pan's periphery. Both species have coarse, spiky leaves, and are virtually inedible to game excepting when young and succulent. However, although neither has any grazing value, *Sporobolus* and *Odyssea* serve an important function in the pan edge ecosystem, forming dense matted swards that trap and collect silt blown off the pan. In this manner they play a major role in raising the fringing soil level above that of the pan surface, thus creating a noticeably less saline environment for colonisation by other not so salt-tolerant plant species.

Once a metre or two of soil has built up, many new plants invade the pan fringe. These include a variety of dwarf shrubs and a host of different grass species, many of which are palatable and nutritious since the substrate on which they grow still contains a high concentration of mineral salts. Along the southern and south-western edge of the Etosha Pan, low-lying plains, which were probably once part of a larger salt pan, stretch for some distance from the present pan edge. The exceptionally sweet grasses that grow on these plains form one of the three major ecological factors that enabled this region to support its famed herds of plains game.

The second factor is the presence of numerous permanent natural springs along, or near, the pan's southern perimeter; whilst the third consists in the vast sandy savanna that extends to the north and north-west of the pan. In combination, these three environmental aspects created the perfect natural grazing system.

In 1876 an American, Gerald McKiernan, travelled around the western edge of the Etosha Pan. In his log he described the scene his party encountered on what is today called Grootvlakte.

"About ten o'clock we came to where there were great numbers of wild animals feeding on the open plain. Gnus, zebra, gemsboks, hartebeeste and thousands of springbok were before us and above the low bush to our left were the long necks of six giraffe. It was the Africa I had read of in books of travel. All the menageries in the world turned loose would not compare to the sight I saw that day."

In the 1950s, when the first nature conservators were stationed within the Etosha Game Park, as it was then called, the plains around the pan still supported over 40 000 head of zebra and wildebeeste, as well as great numbers of springbok, eland, gemsbok and hartebeeste.

This relatively small and arid area was capable of sustaining such large herds of grazing game without major degradation of its sweet and vulnerable grasslands as a result of natural migrations. Since the open tree and scrub savannas to the north and west of the pan are totally devoid of natural springs, the plains game would, in the past, have had to spend most of the dry season along its southern edge, where the herds apparently worked their way slowly from waterhole to waterhole in an eastward direction, grazing as they went on the now dry, but still nutritious, grasses. The great herds would have left little edible grass in their wake; but, once matured and seeded, grass is not adversely affected even by complete defoliation, and thus the production potential of the sweet grasslands would not have been impaired.

In most years, late September would have found the major concentrations of plains game in the vicinity of Namutoni and some thirty kilometres to the north, on the broad treeless Andoni plains, but with the season's first heavy rainfalls a new migration would commence. Following the edge of the pan, the great herds would first have streamed north and then westward onto the sour savannas of southern Ovamboland, where they would have sought out veld recently fire-swept which after rainfall had produced a green flush of succulent new growth. Once the rains started, water would also have been plentiful. Although permanent springs do not occur, scattered throughout the region there are numerous depressions, both large and small, that fill rapidly, providing a supply of rainwater for the duration of the wet season.

The rains in Namibia start in the north-east, moving gradually westward across the country as the season progresses. In Etosha, the migrating plains game followed the pattern of rain across the north of the pan until the drying up of seasonal rainwater pans forced them to trek down Etosha's western edge to the permanent springs around Okaukuejo. From there they retraced their winter arc along the pan's southern rim. The cycle was perfect and productive, for by the time the herds returned to their winter grazing grounds, the sweet grasses were ripe with rippling waves of tawny seed.

This annual migration around the Etosha Pan not only held advantages for the region's grasslands; the game also benefited in many ways. Predators were forced to follow the herds in order to survive, and many young lions, unable to keep up with nomadic prides, would have left their bones to be picked by vultures. The few big cats that chose to stay permanently around the springs would have endured hard times during the wet season and they too would have lost many cubs. Continual movement to fresh pastures moreover prevented the spores of endemic diseases from building up to epidemic proportions.

In 1962 the Odendaal Commission was appointed by the South African government to "further promote the material and moral welfare, and social progress of the inhabitants of South West Africa". Whatever merits this Commission may have had, it unfortunately did not include the promotion of nature conservation, for, when the report was finally published, nature lovers throughout Southern Africa were appalled to find that the Etosha Game Park was to be cut to less than half its existing size. The new Etosha National Park would, in fact, cover less than one third the size of Game Reserve No. 2 as proclaimed by Governor von Lindequist in 1907.

Apart from the deproclamation of the entire Kaokoveld, excepting the desert coast (which became the new Skeleton Coast Park), the most serious set-back to conservation came about with the re-aligning of the Etosha's northern border a few kilometres southwards. Although the actual area excised was relatively small, it brought the Park's boundary to the edge of the pan, which meant that traditional wet-season grazing grounds now had no conservation status. Furthermore, in the early 1970s rampant poaching in southern Ovamboland necessitated the fencing of the northern border, which effectively closed the ancient migration routes. At the time, even the Park's administrators did not fully comprehend what a devastating effect this fence would have on Etosha's ecology.

With the northern savannas no longer available, the great herds were forced to migrate back along the pan's southern rim, grazing the vulnerable plains grasses while they were still growing. This over-taxed the tufts and also used up much of the forage needed to see grass-eating animals through the long dry season. To compound the problem, roads, firebreaks and an active fire control policy suppressed the natural fire regime and further reduced the area of suitable grazing by allowing the sour western grasslands to become moribund and unpalatable, as well as encouraging bush encroachment onto the plains.

Due to the combination of factors related to changed migrational patterns and consequent degradation of the plains grasslands, the resident populations of both wildebeeste and zebra have declined dramatically in recent years. Furthermore, as if to emphasise nature's complexity to the biologists now grappling with these problems, the numbers of other, non-grazing species, have also fallen. Eland, formerly one of the characteristic species of Etosha, are now seldom seen, while the Cape hunting dog, once the most common predator in the pan vicinity, has decreased to at most two small packs that wander in and out of the north-east and north-west of the Park respectively. Cheetah have also decreased in number over the past decade.

The reasons for the decline of a protected species are complex, but basically it is due to adverse changes in habitat. In the case of wildebeeste and zebra in Etosha, ecological studies have shown that the mortalities have largely been due to an endemic animal disease caused by bacteria that have built up at certain artificial waterpoints from where they now cause annual epidemics. However, the downgrading of the park's open grasslands, due to the recently restricted migration patterns of Etosha's plains game, may be the underlying cause.

Although primarily browsers, eland also seem to require their habitat to be burned periodically to maintain trees and shrubs at a young and nutritious growth stage. The artifically depressed fire regime has undoubtedly played a role in their decline, as have the new boundary fences, for eland are normally wide-ranging antelopes that are known to be susceptible to both predation and parasites when their natural range is limited.

Wild dog, once common throughout Southern Africa, is now one of the most endangered species on the sub-continent. Very little about their ecology is known, however, excepting that of all the predators, they are by habit the best adapted to follow migrating herds of plains game, and their demise must likewise be linked to the northern boundary fence. Cheetah, too, seem to adapt easily to a nomadic existence, but in the present situation, where lions dominate all permanent waterholes on the plains, they have suffered heavily from predation by these larger cats who frequently go out of their way to attack and kill potential competitors.

Etosha has always had lions, but in the past the prides were made up of lean and hungry animals, forced to spend much of the year following the herds around the pan. Today the great tawny cats merely laze around the waterholes assured that, for all but a few months at the height of the rains, they need only wait for dinner to arrive 'on the hoof'. Over the last decade every permanent water point along the southern edge of the pan has come to support a resident lion pride and, as cub survival increased, it soon became commonplace to see twenty or more individuals reclining leisurely under the spreading crowns of acacia or buffalo-thorn trees.

Clearly, this abnormally high lion population in the tourist area, coupled with the fact that they are so easily seen on the open grass plains, has contributed much to Etosha's fame. Recently, however, their excessive numbers, particularly in the Okaukuejo and Halali areas, have become a problem, for apart from suppressing other predator populations, it is suspected that they might also be inhibiting the recovery of wildebeeste and plains zebra. Research is currently under way, and a unique control measure — the administering of contraceptive drugs to lionesses — is being tested in Etosha.

Although much of the area now open to visitors in Etosha comprises open plains, this habitat type in fact makes up only a small percentage of the Park's total area. In the south and west are vast tracts of dry savanna; and it is here, often well out of the public eye, that many of Etosha's remarkable success stories have taken place.

Savanna is an amorphous term used to describe a wide range of habitats consisting of both grass and woody vegetation. In Namibia, one or other form of savanna predominates over all the major regions excepting the Namib desert, for wherever there is sufficient rainfall for woody plants to grow they will flourish, unless suppressed by non-climatic factors such as fire, periodic waterlogging or a highly saline substrate.

In Etosha, the savannas are, however, generally low and scrubby, for nowhere in this Park does average rainfall exceed 500 mm. Other environmental factors also influence the nature of savanna and dictate the species of trees, shrubs

and grass that occur. These include soil texture, depth and chemical composition, the underground water table, the frequency of frost and, when abnormally high, the grazing or browsing pressure of herbivorous animals.

Excluding the barren pan surface, over 80% of Etosha's savanna is dominated by a single remarkable tree: the mopane (*Colophospermum mopane*). This hardy species thrives on clayey calcareous soils and predominates over a broad belt across Southern Africa. Where the rainfall or watertable is relatively high, mopane grow into tall, sturdy trees and form woodlands that take on a rich colouration, particularly in winter when their characteristic bi-lobed 'butterfly' leaves turn to fiery shades of rust and amber.

The mopane is remarkably resilient to veld fires. With small trees this fire tolerance is achieved by vigorous coppicing from the roots after a blaze, but as they grow taller the trees develop a thick corky bark that protects their inner heat-sensitive tissue from the flames. Once a mopane has reached a height of about three metres it will remain unscathed by all but the hottest fire, enabling the species to dominate vast tracts of periodically burned veld.

The mopane, however, does have an Achilles heel — sensitivity to frost; and where sub-zero night temperatures frequently occur, they cannot become established. Light or infrequent frosting creates one of the mopane's most typical growth forms — low, untidy shrubs, commonly referred to as 'scrub mopane'.

In spring, when the drab winter stems of the mopane burst into delicate apple-green leaf, many different animals feed upon the soft, almost translucent new buds; but as they grow, mopane leaves quickly become coarse, fibrous and very high in turpentine, making them unpalatable to the majority of browsing game. In Etosha, only eland and elephant seem to utilize significant quantities of mature mopane leaves. Elephant are moreover particularly fond of young mopane bark. This species thus provides the bulk of the pachyderms' diet in all seasons excepting when fire and rain have produced a flush of new green grass.

Under natural conditions in Africa, elephants range over vast areas; and in Namibia their domain once extended down to the Orange River in the far south, and, where there were large riverbeds, deep into the Namib. Notwithstanding their great size and prodigious strength, elephants are peace-loving creatures that seldom seek confrontation excepting in defence of their young. Nevertheless wherever Africa has been 'tamed', elephant have been ruthlessly exterminated — a bloody persecution undertaken to provide wealthy Europeans with mounted tusks, carved ornaments, billiard balls and creamy white piano keys.

By the end of the 19th century, Namibia's elephants seemed well on the road to extinction. Even after protective legislation had been introduced, a comprehensive mammal survey conducted by Shortridge in 1934 found that the only regions where relatively large numbers of elephant still survived were the Kaokoveld and Eastern Caprivi. Shortridge recorded no elephant at all in the vicinity of the Etosha Pan, and only small wandering herds in any part of the present National Park, east of Otjovasandu. However, after the appointment of full-time conservation staff, elephant numbers steadily built up and recent surveys have indicated a total population in excess of 2 500, spread throughout the Park.

Apart from strict protection, undoubtedly the major factor contributing to the elephants' dramatic recovery has been the creation of numerous artificial waterpoints that have greatly extended the elephants' dry season range in Etosha. Immigration from outside the Park's boundaries — where poaching still continues — has also played a role.

After more than a century of relentless hunting, Namibia's elephants have at last found a sanctuary but, ironically, their rapid population growth within the present confines of the Park has created a grim situation where the very conservators who fought and sometimes risked their lives to protect them, must now contemplate some form of population control in order to prevent elephants from degrading their habitat.

The black or hook-lipped rhinoceros is another species once common and widespread in Namibia that has been saved from the brink of extinction in the Etosha Park. By the late 1960s the Kaokoveld remained the last rhino stronghold, but this area had been deprived of its conservation status by the Odendaal Commission. As a result of this situation, 54 of these endangered animals were captured and successfully translocated to Etosha. Today there are probably more black rhino in Etosha than at any time in the recent past, for they, like other browsing species such as giraffe, kudu and black-faced impala, have thrived on the abundant supply of shrubs and trees that have sprung up as a result of the reduced burning frequency in the Park. This however added another complicating factor to the already complex management problems facing the Park's administrators.

When the first conservators and biologists were appointed in Etosha, it was their unwritten policy to maintain the Park in as pristine a state as possible and human interference was therefore reduced to an absolute minimum. However, fencing the Park boundaries and creating roads, which acted as fire-breaks for natural fires, had a considerable effect on the ecosystem whilst other worthy undertakings, such as the provision of new permanent waterpoints and the active combating of veld fires, unbalanced the natural ecology of the region still further. Even prohibiting the Heikum Bushmen from practising their only traditional trade in this area has had an effect, for these primitive hunters were part of the Etosha ecosystem for thousands of years, playing a role in the control of certain animal populations.

Throughout Africa, National Parks administrators have been forced to accept that it is not enough just to proclaim an area for conservation and then 'leave it to nature'. All Parks are undersized, simply because artificial boundaries have been imposed upon the natural ecosystem. Consequently man's every action within a Park must now be balanced by deliberate management practices.

The drama of Etosha is ageless, for since time immemorial the great herds of game have followed the rhythmic beat of the seasons along its shimmering shore. Slowly, inexorably, the pan as we know it today is shrinking and one day, in the far distant future, the creeping sands will encroach over the last few metres of Etosha's saline clay surface. Man will play no part in this momentous geological event but it will be his actions alone that determine whether there are still elephant, wildebeeste and lion there to witness it.

In the Etosha National Park disputes
within a lion pride are settled savagely.
These conflicts are not intended
to cause serious injury, however,
and are rarely prolonged.

Many permanent waterholes
in the eastern part of the Park
are dominated by large groups of lion,
often to the detriment of other
predators, such as cheetah.
The abnormally high lion population
may also be suppressing
the recovery of wildebeeste and plains zebra.
Current research on lions in Etosha
includes the testing of
contraceptive drugs on lionesses,
which, if they prove effective,
may be instituted in the future,
rather than a culling programme,
to combat the problems
of overpopulation.

Left: A steenbok doe peers inquisitively through the Etosha bush.

Previous page:
A gemsbok herd stands quietly before the Kapupuhedi waterhole at the edge of the vast saline desert that comprises the Etosha Pan.

117

Left: At one time rarely seen in the Etosha, giraffe have in recent years
benefited from the increase of thorn bush cover and are today common in the Park.
Giraffe can go for prolonged periods without water,
which enables them to utilize
waterless tracts of the Etosha which are beyond the range of other browsers.

Above: Martial eagles are the largest raptors in Etosha where they feed primarily on guinea fowl.

Below: Damara dikdik are the smallest of all antelopes in Namibia.
They frequent dry wooded areas of the north west.

Right: Common resident of the Etosha's open plains, yellow mongooses live in
burrows which are frequently shared with ground squirrels.

Overleaf: An elephant herd makes its way leisurely towards the Goas waterhole.

An elephant group finds respite from the midday sun at Rietfontein,
a waterhole in the central part of Etosha.
Elephants are very sociable animals and may congregate in groups
of up to fifty in Etosha, but these large herds are not stable,
seldom remaining together for more than a few weeks.
More permanent family groups usually contain five to fifteen members.
At the end of the 19th century no elephant were recorded
in the vicinity of the Etosha Pan, but the creation of
artificial waterpoints and the appointment of full-time conservation
staff have enabled the elephant population to flourish
until today the possibility of elephant overpopulation could cause
a serious problem in Etosha.

Opposite: A lone bull elephant coated with pale dust from the Etosha Pan.
This habit of spraying themselves with dust or mud
is thought to protect the sensitive parts of the skin against insect bites.

Overleaf:
Above: Zebra are gregarious animals
and generally congregate in the large herds at waterholes where,
during the hot dry months, they must drink daily.

Below: Permanent springs and sweet grasslands
at the southern edge of the Etosha Pan attract large herds of
plains game during the dry season.

A solitary zebra stallion stands hock-deep amidst dry but nutritious grass.

Opposite: For zebra the slightest disturbance at a waterhole usually precipitates panic.

A fine young kudu bull. These magnificent antelopes occur throughout Namibia wherever water and suitable browse is available.

Above: Migratory by habit, springbok can gather in herds of up to 5 000 in the Etosha when rains produce a flush of rich new grass on the western plains.

Below, left: Young warthogs 'on the trot'.

Below, right: Cheetah are today scarce in the Etosha due to predation by lions that have been observed to kill cheetah who encroach on their territory.

Overleaf, left: The rare black-faced impala formerly occurred only in northern Kaokoland; but in recent years they have been exterminated in this region as a result of uncontrolled hunting. Fortunately, however, during 1969-70 small numbers were introduced into central Etosha where today they are thriving.

Right: Ground squirrels are sociable diurnal creatures of the Etosha plains where they feed upon vegetable matter, especially bulbs, roots and the leaves of small shrubs.

Above: Red-billed queleas frequently move about in enormous flocks,
synchronising their movements with uncanny precision.
In Etosha queleas provide food for a variety of small raptors.

Previous page:
Left, above: A swallow-tailed bee-eater rests momentarily on a slender twig.
Agile and acrobatic in the air, these small birds catch their insect prey on the wing.

Far left, below: Today threatened by hunting over much of Southern Africa,
Kori bustards in Etosha are characteristic birds of the open grasslands.

Centre, below: Crimson-breasted shrikes prefer the more wooded areas
of Etosha where they forage on the ground for small invertebrates.

Right: A yellow-billed hornbill perches on a broken tree stump.

Above: White pelicans cruise the saline waters of
Fischer's Pan, an extension of the Etosha Pan.
During years of good rainfall, parts of the pan system
are flooded, attracting great numbers of waterbirds.

Below: Grey loeries, commonly known as "Go'way birds",
gather at an Etosha waterhole.

A bush squirrel nibbles
on the blossom of *Acacia hebeclada*.
Before the onset of
summer rains acacia blossoms
form an important food source
for many animal species
ranging from squirrel
to giraffe and rhinoceros.

Previous page:
Left, above: Crenellated patterns
of mud on the sun-baked surface
of the Etosha Pan.

Left, Below: Rock strata of
contrasting dolomite and mudstone.

Right: A lilac-breasted roller
surveys the veld from the slender
stem of a dwarf shrub.

Overleaf: As the pale winter sun
sinks towards the horizon,
a herd of wildebeest grazes
peacefully on the grassy plains.

The rugged Northwest: Skeleton coast to mountainous bastion

The remote and virtually inaccessible Kaokoveld has for long been a land of legend and mystery. Its rugged scenery, fascinating peoples and exceptional wildlife often evoked romantic tales and wild speculation from the privileged few who breached the strict security regulations that, until recently, prohibited entry into the region.

The first White man to attempt to penetrate the Kaokoveld interior was Charles Andersson, while in search of the Kunene River. In 1858 Andersson set off from Otjimbingwe on the central plateau, and after trekking with difficulty across its broad plains, he was confronted by a spectacular mountain range.

"It presented the finest and most peculiar hill-scenery I have ever seen. For upwards of fifty miles it formed a perfect table, with perpendicular side cliffs, many hundred feet high. Towards its western extremity, the range was broken into detached 'tables', as beauteous and varied in aspect as can possibly be conceived. There were extensive fortifications with gigantic buttresses exquisitely 'worked' in all their details; crumbling pieces of Gothic architecture, with all the delicate outlines, touches, characteristics, and finish of that beautiful art; splendid Italian villas, with terrace-like slopes besprinkled with decaying sculptures, variegated marbles, huge sepuchral-like caverns, stuccoed grottoes, and many other singular and pageant forms.

"At the foot of this interesting range, a noble periodical watercourse shaped its way, its banks clothed with a rich verdure of every hue, whilst here and there sprang up stately groups of acacias, interspersed with pleasant shrubs and sweet-smelling plants. Grass also, of the rankest and most luxuriant description, frangrant with odours, reached, as they laboured along with the huge and cumbersome vehicle behind them, the oxen's bellies. In the background and indeed almost everywhere around us, the scene was bounded by extensive and lofty mountain ranges.

"When yet at a distance I had carefully reconnoitred this range through the telescope; and when sufficiently near to scan it with the naked eye, had anxiously pried into its every crevice, every cranny, every slight indentation, in the hope of finding some break or opening to get across the mountain; all in vain."

Andersson had reached the Kaokoveld: but after more than a month of toil and anguish, he had to admit defeat. By then he had penetrated some distance, but lack of water and the interminable mountain ranges forced him to retrace his steps and seek a different route, further to the east. In so doing he discovered the Okavango River. Nine more years elapsed before the explorer finally stood on the Kunene's reed-fringed banks, but by this time the many years of hardship and deprivation had broken his health, and it had only been tremendous courage and an indomitable spirit that kept him true to his quest. A few days later, at the age of forty, Andersson died and was buried just south of the river that he had sought with such determination for seventeen years.

One of the most remarkable exploratory journeys in the Kaokoveld was undertaken by a group of four Boers under Gert Alberts, in the year 1878. Travelling light, on horseback, they traversed the entire Kaokoveld from east to west, reaching Rotsfort (Rocky Point) on the Skeleton Coast. Unencumbered by wagons, Alberts and his companions managed to negotiate the Kaokoveld's formidable mountains with relative ease and, by following the courses of large seasonal rivers, they obtained sufficient water for their frugal needs. Subsequent to this reconnaissance, a large party of Boers moved to Otjitundua and Kaoko Otavi, springs in the eastern Kaokoveld, where they remained for two years before crossing the Kunene River and settling in southern Angola.

The Boers who sojourned in the Kaokoveld never forgot the great herds of elephants they had encountered and some of them returned to hunt these animals year after year. Jan Robbertse was reputed to be the most successful of these ivory hunters. Every winter for twenty eight years Robbertse and his associates set up a large camp on the banks of the Kunene from where they ranged far and wide into the Kaokoveld and adjoining areas of south-western Angola. In return for meat, the Herero tribesmen, impoverished as a result of frequent raids by bands of Topnaar and Swartbooi Nama, willlingly guided the Boers to where the largest elephant concentrations were to be found. The Herero moreover acted as informers, keeping the hunters aware of police activites in the area, for after 1892 the hunting of elephant in Namibia without permission from the German Governor had been made illegal.

1900 was Robbertse's most successful year, when a total of 182 elephant were killed in the Kaokoveld, most of them illegally. In 1907, however, the Kaokoveld was proclaimed a game reserve, and two years later, after a few close shaves with the German authorities, Robbertse finally decided to quit. During his years in the bush he and his fellow hunters had killed over 2 000 elephants. From the profits of this carnage he purchased nine farms in the Transvaal.

In 1911 a different kind of explorer arrived in the Kaokoveld. Whilst the Boers had been motivated by economic or territorial incentives, and Andersson by the fame attached to new geographical discoveries, Maudslay Baynes, a young Scot, was driven only by the call of adventure. At this time, much of the southern and eastern Kaokoveld had been well explored, but there were still large tracts in the far north that were just blank spaces on the map. Nothing at all was known of the Kunene River's course between its upper and lower reaches, north of Ovamboland, and its mouth, which had been visited by the geologist Georg Hartmann in 1896.

Unannounced and without companions, Baynes set off towards the Kunene which he reached at Erikson's Drift in Angola. From here he followed the course of the river downstream, passing through some of the most spectacular mountain scenery in Southern Africa before finally emerging onto the coastal plain, 500 kilometres and 93 days later. The modest and unassuming Baynes told few people of his epic trip — in fact, it might never have been recorded had he not chanced to meet Dr. Kuntz, a German geologist and land-surveyor, while travelling by train to Swakopmund on his way home to Scotland. As a result of this encounter, the port authorities at Swakopmund, undoubtedly prompted by Kuntz, opened Baynes' luggage and examined his notes. The Germans did however give Baynes the credit for his discoveries, and a few years later the young Scot was astonished to see, on the latest German map of the territory, his name across the great mountain range that he had been the first European to view.

The magnitude of Baynes' achievement can be appreciated by tracing the course of the Kunene River as it wends its way through valleys, sheer gorges and massive desert dunes before finally disgorging into the Atlantic on the desolate Skeleton Coast.

In Angola, where Baynes commenced his journey, the Kunene is a broad sluggish waterway that during peak floods may reach over two kilometres across. Shortly before reaching the international border however, its pace quickens and for 30 kilometres the river cascades over a series of foaming rapids that convey it to the lip of the mighty Ruacana waterfall, at which point it makes a dramatic entrance into Namibia, by plunging 100 metres into a great chasm.

The fast-flowing stretch of river between Ruacana and the Epupa Falls, 170 kilometres to the west, is studded with numerous islands, all but the smallest supporting a rich riparian growth dominated by majestic sycamore figs, baobabs, ana trees, ebonies, leadwoods and tall mopane. Similar vegetation fringes the river's actual banks, here enhanced by groves of stately *makalani* palms. The Zebra Mountains now come into view: an extraordinary range of high ridges and conical peaks whose steep slopes are characterised by vertical bands of loosely piled black boulders that contrast with broader belts of low matted bush, giving the mountains a strange striped appearance.

At Epupa the bed of the Kunene is once again slashed by a deep cataract. Here the main stream disappears entirely into a narrow fissure that, although a mere eight metres across, is over forty metres deep. When in full flood, the river divides into many channels, creating a wonderland of cascading water.

Below the Epupa Falls, the character of the Kunene changes completely. No more the gentle meanders of its upper reaches, or the verdant banks and sparkling white waters that distinguished its course through the Zebra Mountains. Ahead lie the Baynes, Shamalindi and Otjihipa ranges, with rugged peaks that tower up to 1 500 metres above the river's turbulent waters. Deep within these mountains, sheer cliffs rear 300 metres straight out of the river, and in places its course is so constricted that in a single night the water level may rise six metres or more.

Until helicopters came into general use, few people had seen the inside of these mighty gorges. Maudslay Baynes had managed to follow the Kunene for some distance into the mountains, but he was eventually forced to make a wide northern detour, 1 000 metres above the river. To this day, only two people, Willem van Riet and Gordon Rowe, have actually traversed the entire canyon at water level using kayaks in 1964. Apart from deadly rapids, the two canoeists had also to contend with crocodiles which repeatedly attacked their flimsy craft. Both men admitted afterwards that the lower Kunene was so daunting that had it been possible for them to leave the river after having entered the gorge, they would willingly have done so. In subsequent years, other canoeists have attempted to conquer the Kunene, but all have come to grief.

The Kunene's exit from the Baynes and Otjihipo Mountains is still more spectacular than its entrance. The great mountains fold back to expose a majestic plain 70 kilometres long and some 20 kilometres broad — completely surrounded by towering walls of rock. "It was like another world," wrote Baynes many years later. So beautiful is this valley that the early German explorers named it the *Marienfluss* in honour of the Virgin Mary.

After traversing the northern end of the *Marienfluss,* the Kunene once more enters rugged mountains, this time the bald granite peaks of the Hartmannberge. By now the river is deep within the Namib desert, its course forming an emerald ribbon that winds through one of the most desolate landscapes on Earth.

As the Kunene approaches the coast, massive sand dunes build up on the south bank to heights of 100 metres or more. To the north, stark and crumbling rock pavements resolve imperceptibly into endless plains of barren gravel. At one point the entire river vanishes beneath huge granite boulders that have collapsed into the water from adjoining cliffs, while at another, the river bed is scored by a series of narrow clefts that form cataracts ten metres high when the river runs low, but fill with water and disappear altogether when it is in flood. The actual mouth of the Kunene is, however, an anti-climax, consisting merely of a long shallow lagoon of brackish water.

South of the Kunene, the Kaokoveld — comprising the present Kaokoland and Damaraland homelands as well as the recently proclaimed Skeleton Coast Park — can be divided geographically into a low-lying coastal plain that rises some 500 metres above sea level, and a mountainous interior plateau ranging from 800 to 2 000 metres, the altitude of the highest mountain peak. Average annual rainfall varies from less than 25 mm on the coast to over 350 mm in the north-east. This, coupled with the great topographic variation, creates an exceptionally wide range of habitats within the region.

Numerous seasonal rivers drain the mountainous Kaokoveld highlands, the largest of which have carved impressive valleys between the brooding ranges. As a result of periodic springs and rich riverine vegetation, these watercourses spread a network of life-supporting arteries through the region. Together with scattered natural artesian fountains, they once sustained the finest wildlife populations in Namibia. For most of this century the Kaokoveld formed a stronghold for both elephant and black rhino while other big game species were still plentiful until very recently.

The Kaokoveld's wildlife was not only numerous and varied, in some cases it was ecologically unique; for in the west of the region a number of large mammals normally associated with warmer climates, occurred deep into the Namib — eking a living from the dry river beds that traversed the parched desert plains. To this day it is still possible to encounter elephant and lion actually on the Skeleton Coast, whilst black rhino and giraffe may be seen within a few kilometres inland of this forbidding shore. It is still not fully understood how these animals are able to survive in this extremely hostile environment.

Some of the most dramatic scenery in the Kaokoveld occurs in the centre of the region. Here the broad valley of the Hoanib River is virtually encircled by rugged limestone ranges that are slashed by sheer precipices and pocked by numerous caves. Sesfontein, a series of artesian springs, from which millions of litres of water gush daily, nestles at the foot of these mountains. Around the springs graceful sycamore figs have grown, creating cool shady glades in stark contrast to the blinding sunshine and sheer rock slopes of the surrounding ranges. At one time Sesfontein must have been a paradise, but long years of occupation by Nama and Herero pastoralists have completely devastated the grass cover, reducing the valley to a dustbowl for most of the year.

Further to the east, at Khowarib, where the Hoanib cuts through the arid mountains, the river has incised a spectacular canyon between massive cliffs. Near the Hoanib's exit from this gorge, water is forced up to the surface of the river bed forming a strong flowing spring that, a mere decade ago, was still regularly frequented by large herds of elephant. Today, odd elephants still visit the spring, as do mountain zebra, but the magnificent spectacle of great herds wending their way leisurely between massive riverine trees beneath the Khowarib's formidable rock krantzes, now survives only in the memory of those who knew the Kaokoveld in its former glory.

A jagged spine of mountains separates the Kaokoveld highlands from the coastal plain. In places this escarpment forms an unbroken wall of warped and shattered rock: a spectacular backdrop to the tawny semi-desert plains in the west of the region. Near the escarpment, the Namib itself is divided into a system of broad valleys by chains of impressive inselbergs. It is only in the far west, as one

approaches the coast, that the topography of the region gradually flattens out into the characteristic gravel plains of the Namib desert.

Few coastlines on earth present so bleak and forbidding an aspect as Namibia's northern shore, known inauspiciously as the Skeleton Coast. Between the mouths of the Ugab and Kunene rivers few significant features relieve the endless succession of bleak beaches that merge gradually into the desolate gravel flats and occasional low rock ridges of the Namib. Regular sea fogs roll in off the Atlantic, shrouding the shore for many kilometres inland and, when they lift, icy winds sweep across the sands.

Apart from its fascinating history of shipwrecks and human drama, the Skeleton coast has considerable biological value. Of particular significance are the small brackish lagoons and pans at the mouths of seasonal rivers that form oases of green; habitat for waterfowl and sustenance for game.

Remarkably, big game animals that are normally associated with Africa's savannas and woodlands occur in this region deep within the Namib desert. Kaokoveld elephants have been seen on the beaches of the Skeleton Coast, and a few small herds appear to live permanently in the lower courses of the Uniab, Hoanib and Hoarusib, frequently crossing the plains that separate these dry river beds.

In the western Kaokoveld, black rhino inhabit the most remote mountain regions, where the only vegetation comprises sparse wiry grass and hardy xerophytic shrubs. Occasionally they are encountered on the barren gravel flats deep within the Namib, a harsh habitat where it appears they are capable of surviving for many days without water.

Giraffe present perhaps the most enchanting picture in the barren desert where trees are so few and far between. Recent studies suggest that in this forbidding environment giraffe might not drink at all, obtaining instead sufficient moisture from their diet of acacia leaves; an astonishing adaptation for so large an animal.

The Kaokoveld lion has been almost exterminated in the interior highlands, but small numbers still survive in the western part of the region. At least one pride appears to be permanently resident within a few kilometres of the coast, and nature conservators in the Skeleton Coast Park have even seen their pug marks on the shore, just above the high-water mark. In 1907, the German colonial government proclaimed four game reserves in Namibia, the second of which, known simply as Game Reserve II, included most of the present Etosha National Park as well as the entire modern Kaokoveld. Its total area embraced over 72 000 square kilometres. In subsequent years, the boundaries of this great reserve were frequently altered — a piece of land taken off here and a bit added there, but nevertheless it remained by far the greatest single conserved area in the world until 1968

when, on the recommendation of the Odendaal Commission, a significant part of the Etosha National Park, as well as most of the Kaokoveld, was deproclaimed. Of the latter, only a 32 kilometre strip of desert along the Skeleton Coast now remains as a game reserve.

The deproclamation of the Kaokoveld as a game reserve caused a concerted outcry from conservationists in Southern Africa and other parts of the world. All pointed out that the new Skeleton Coast Park was ecologically incapable of providing sanctuary for the larger game animals of this region which, with few exceptions, were dependant on feeding grounds further inland. Without legal protection here, these species would inevitably be doomed. In response, the South African government made promises to undertake alternative arrangements to ensure protection of the Kaokoveld fauna and flora; but to date not one of these promises has been kept.

The past decade has brought about far-reaching changes in the Kaokoveld. During this period, the once magnificent wildlife of the region has been decimated, and today only small remnant populations survive. In some cases, the numbers of certain species are already so low that they are probably unviable. Unless action is taken immediately, the ecologically unique Kaokoveld elephant, black rhino and giraffe will become extinct.

Near Torra Bay,
the notorious 'Skeleton Coast'
presents a wild
rugged seascape.

Overleaf: For most of
its course through the Namib
Desert the Huab River
flows underground, but near
the coast, rock formations
force the water to
surface again.

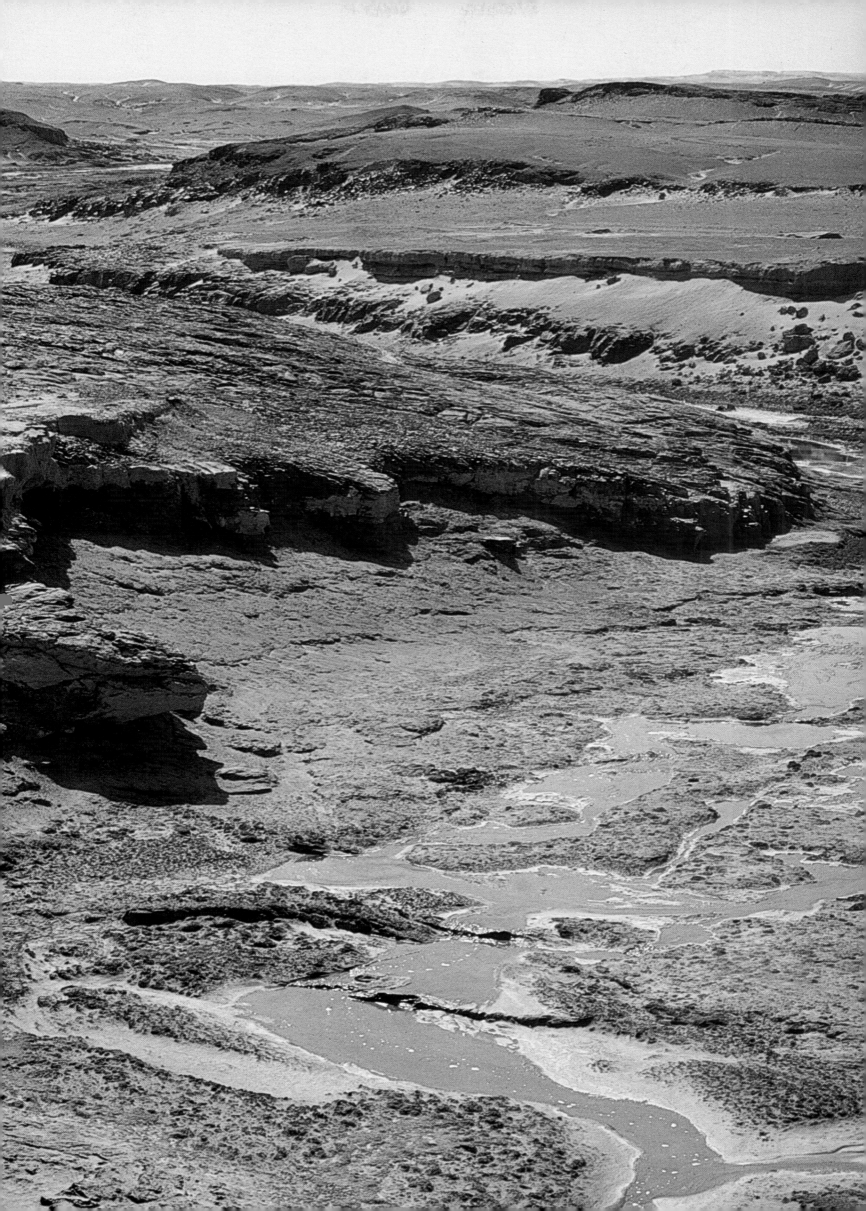

A flight of greater flamingoes keeps close formation over the Skeleton Coast.
Right, above: Wind-blasted granite outcrops give a distinctive character
to the desert near the Uniab River mouth.
Right, below: The skeletal remains of a cormorant, graceful even in death.

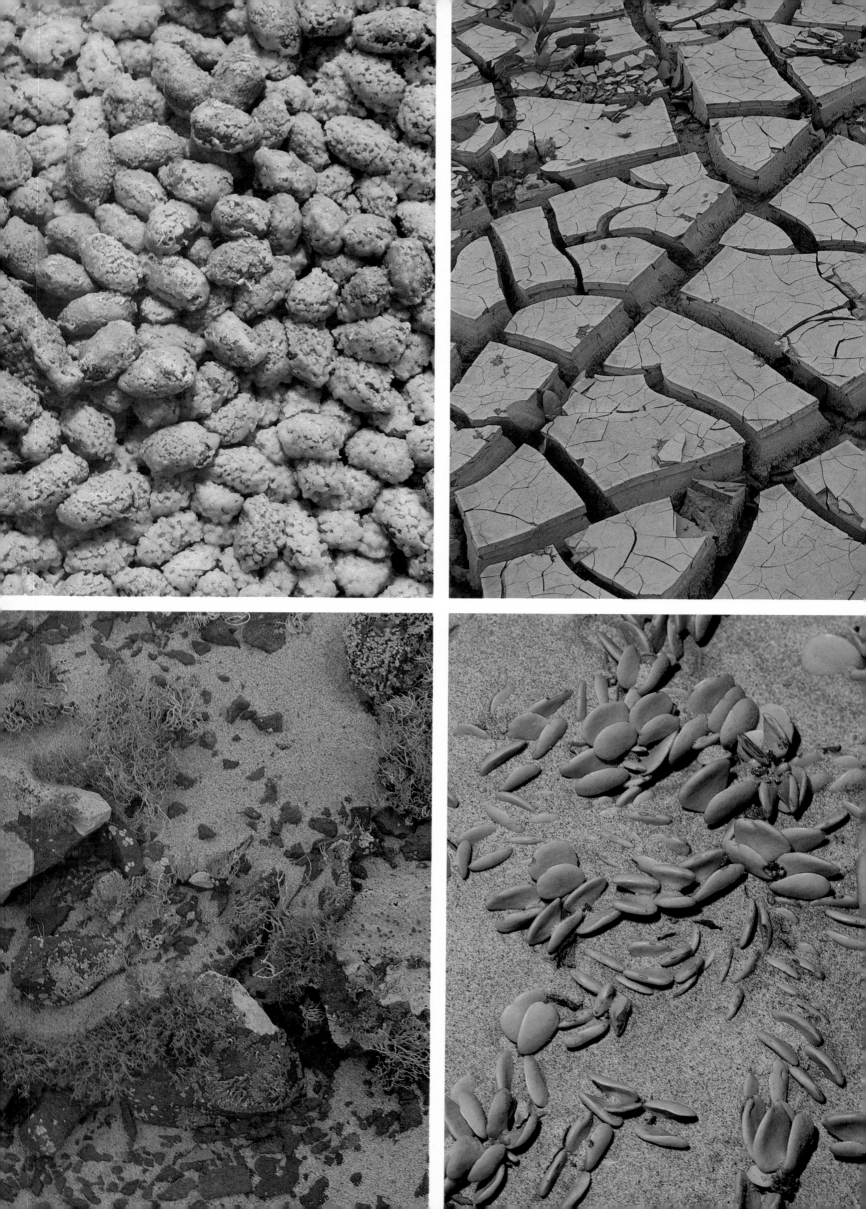

Gnarled mopane trees cling
tenaciously to the banks of the Hoanib River
in the *Khowarib Schlucht*.

Previous page:
Left, above: Springbok droppings
encrusted with salt from a saline spring in the
lower reaches of the Hoanib River.

Left, below: Sustained by moisture
carried on the prevailing south-westerly wind,
desert stones support
three different forms of lichen:
crustose (scale-like), foliose (leafy)
and fruticose (branched, grey-green and orange).

Centre, above: Cracked mud patterns
in the dry bed of the Ugab River.

Centre, below: Partly covered by desert sand,
the succulent leaves of
the dollar bush *(Zygophyllum stapfii)*
are a common feature of the
northern Skeleton Coast.

Right: *Helichrysum roseo-niveum,*
an endemic 'everlasting' of the northern coast.

Overleaf:
The Hoanib River valley, near Sesfontein
in northern Damaraland.

Pseudogaltonia clavata, a poisonous veld plant known as 'snake's head'.

Sunlight filtered
through a haze of dust
in tall acacia woodland.

Above: *Sesamum schinzianum*

Right: The Hoaníb River, southern boundary of Kaokoland,
flows only during the rainy season.
In the spectacular Khowaríb Gorge however, owing to an abundance of
water from springs and seepage, the river banks
support a rich vegetation of dense green thickets and towering trees,
which appears almost lush by comparison with the usual
scrubby woodland of this region.

Above: Landscape in the Kamanjab district.

Below: A massive pillar of consolidated sediment, a relic of silt deposited on the floor of an ancient lake.

Previous page, left: A small group of Hartmann's mountain zebra beside the dry Uniab River is dwarfed by a sere landscape of red boulders and green euphorbia bushes.

Right: Formerly widespread throughout the arid wilderness of north-western Namibia, today elephants in Damaraland are reduced to small family groups in the more inaccessible regions.

Pachypodium lealii, commonly called 'elephant's foot', is an ubiquitous
plant in many parts of Damaraland.

Overleaf:
Left, above: *Euphorbia virosa* on a rock-strewn plateau.
Left, below: A curiously stunted growth of *Pachypodium lealii.*
Right: A black rhinoceros and calf stand amidst a strange environment
of 'milk bush' succulents (*Euphorbia gregarii*) and red boulders.
Rhinoceros of the arid western sector of Damaraland and Kaokoland are considered
ecologically unique in view of their specialized adaptation to semi-desert conditions.

An austere landscape of
dry thorny savanna typical
of northern Kaokoland.

Previous pages:
Sunset from Palmwag
on the Uniab River.

The remote Kaokoveld
covers a vast area of
north-western Namibia.
Until recently access to
the region was restricted,
but even today the
rough mountainous terrain
and insufficiency
of water have maintained
a natural barrier
to man's endeavours.

Above: At Epupa
the bed of the Kunene
is slashed by a
deep cataract.

Below: At the base
of the Epupa Falls
the Kunene flows
through a narrow
gorge on its
course to the Atlantic.

Opposite: Beside
the Kunene River
the exposed roots of
a baobab are
anchored tightly
to rocky fissures.

Overleaf:
Flowing placidly
through the parched
and arid Kaokoland,
the Kunene brings
abundant life
to its banks.

175

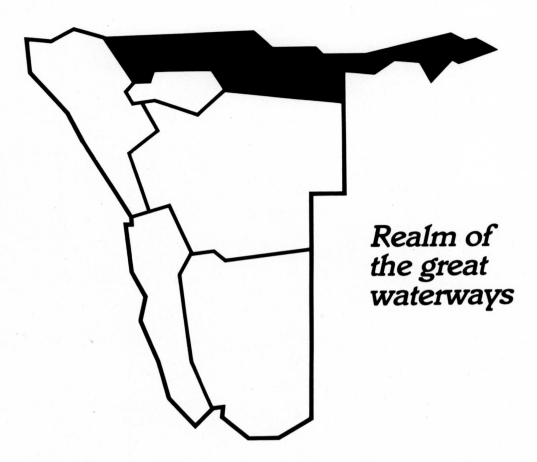

Realm of the great waterways

Stealthily the soft dawn steals through quiescent riverine vegetation and gently touches the glassy surface of a reed-fringed waterway. The crisp night air has precipitated a shroud of pale mist that lingers lightly on the silvery stream. No creature stirs, and the tranquillity of the scene is disturbed only by the slow drift of floating waterweed and the gentle rocking of a broken reed stem, caught in the sluggish current.

The faint chatter of awakening birds steadily swells, paying homage to the new day. Bulbuls, barbets, grey loeries and doves add their distinctive calls to the raucous chatter of babblers. From deep within the reeds come weird growls and purrs, strange calls of seldom-seen swamp birds joining the rising crescendo of sound. Far in the distance a hippo grunts and another, much closer, answers.

Slowly, majestically, the tropical sun rises, transforming the stagnant shallows into pools of liquid gold and sending shafts of orange light stabbing between the riverbank trees to tint the swirling mist and paint delicate colours onto the tightly packed reeds. The first flights of whistling duck, teal and hadeda ibis wing across the water towards distant rendezvous, and from a long-dead wild fig a pair of fish eagles rend the morning air with a duet of echoing cries.

A slight, ebony-skinned man arrives at the water's edge where he squats beside a heavy dugout canoe gazing intently out over the smooth water. Presently the huge head of a hippo, only just visible through the rising mist, quietly breaks the surface, ejects a vaporous jet of air through flared nostrils, and as silently disappears back beneath the water. The man continues to watch until satisfied that only one of the great beasts lurks in this part of the river. He awaits the moment when the hippo submerges and then expertly propels his craft across the stream. By the time the great head surfaces once more, the man is safely against the reeds on the far bank. Here, as the sun's warm rays melt the last wisps of mist off the water, he works his way steadily along a line of fish nets, checking the night's catch.

This simple rural scene has been enacted every day for many centuries along the waterways that form much of Namibia's north-eastern border. The region they bound comprises less than 20% of the Territory's land surface, but supports over 60% of the population — a fact all the more remarkable because much of it is waterless Kalahari. These great rivers and their fertile floodplains are the key.

Beyond the Etosha Pan lies an immense flat sand-plain which stretches northwards 130 kilometres to Namibia's border with Angola, and for nearly 1 000 kilometres from western Ovamboland to the eastern tip of the Caprivi strip.

This region is part of the great Kalahari Basin, the largest continuous mantle of deep sand on the Earth's surface. In Namibia alone, Kalahari sands overlie more than 200 000 square kilometres; but this vast system also covers most of Botswana and spreads into four adjacent countries: Angola, Zambia, Zimbabwe and South Africa. The total surface of the Kalahari is over two and a half million square kilometres in extent, and in places the loose sands lie more than 1 000 metres deep.

The Kalahari sands originated as coarse sediments carried by ancient rivers and deposited in an enormous lake and swamp system that many millions of years ago covered much of what is now Southern Africa. Today only remnants of this great wetland survive, supporting arid woodland, savanna or scrub. These pockets are separated by vast tracts of parched and waterless sandveld, criss-crossed by dry channels that once carried surging floods, but now contain water only when summer rainfall raises the water-table above the level of their turf beds. Since they are periodically waterlogged, trees cannot grow along these fossil waterways

but the high water-table provides an ideal habitat for the growth of lush grassland.

Compared to the rest of the country the north-east of Namibia is favoured by an almost extravagant rainfall that generally exceeds 500 mm per annum — ample under normal conditions to support dry-land grain crops such as maize, sorghum and millet.

Ironically, the Kalahari's deep, thirsty sands greedily soak in the falling rain which rapidly infiltrates through the loose grains to depths well beyond the reach of even the hardiest crops. What little remains in the upper soil layers is quickly baked out by the blazing sun. However, although the rain that falls over much of the northern Kalahari is of little use to man, and provides only temporary rain-filled pans for the scattered herds of game, parts of the region do in fact support agriculture that is sustained not by rain but by flood-waters from mighty rivers that rise on the central highlands of Angola.

Ovamboland is today by far the most densely populated part of Namibia. Although it comprises only 8% of the Territory's land surface, nearly half the total human population resides here. The effect of this high population density on the landscape has been considerable. The tall woodlands that once fringed the muddy oshanas (seasonally flooded pans) have long since been cut down to provide firewood and building materials for intricately palisaded Ovambo homesteads, while overgrazing along the major waterways has turned large tracts of once luxuriant grassland into a barren dustbowl for up to eight months of the year. Game has disappeared from all but the lightly inhabited south and east of the region. Nevertheless, the well-tilled plains of Ovambo, dotted with tall *makalani* palms, massive wild fig, marula and other traditionally protected fruit trees, still present some of the most pleasant scenery in Namibia. When the annual *efundja* floodwater spreads its sparkling blue tentacles across the landscape, the arid plains are miraculously transformed into a watery paradise that attracts great flocks of pelicans, flamingoes, ibis, storks and countless waterfowl.

A high rain-drenched plateau in Angola's central highlands, a few hundred kilometres from Namibia's northern border, gives rise to virtually all the major river systems in south-central Africa. Here, literally within a few kilometres of one another, rise the Kunene, Okavango, Kwito, Kuanza and Zambesi Rivers. Remarkably, although this great watershed is situated a mere 400 kilometres from the Atlantic coast, all but the Kunene strike out not westward but east, towards a seashore more than 3 000 kilometres distant. Only the mighty Zambesi, however, successfully traverses the sub-continent to deliver its olive green waters, conceived of mist and rain from those far-off Angolan peaks, into the warm Indian Ocean off Mozambique.

Of all Africa's rivers south of the Congo, the Okavango is second only to the Zambesi when measured in terms of annual water flow. By the time it reaches the Namibian border north east of Nkurenkuru, the Okavango has already flowed more than 600 kilometres from its mountain source, and has matured into a flat, strongly flowing waterway. In places the river splits into three or four tree-lined channels, but more frequently it forms a single broad expanse of shimmering blue water that surges with quiet determination towards the great swamplands of north-eastern Botswana. At

this point the river disappears into a great sea of *Phragmites* and papyrus from which only two minor streams emerge — one spasmodically feeding the moribund Lake Ngami, and the other winding tortuously for another 400 kilometres across the Kalahari's sandy wastes before spewing a shallow veneer of tepid fluid over the burning surface of the Makarikari salt pans in the heart of the desert.

The first White man to set eyes on the Okavango River was Charles John Andersson in 1858. At the time, the presence of this river was not even suspected in Europe and Andersson was in fact searching for the upper reaches of the Kunene — a river whose mouth had been charted centuries before by Portuguese mariners exploring the Atlantic coast. After almost a year of wandering, Andersson finally stood on the banks of a broad, strongly flowing river which he first believed to be the object of his quest. It was only after gazing at the scene for a few moments that he realized to his utter dismay that instead of the water flowing westward, to empty itself into the Atlantic, the river in fact ran east —towards the very heart of the continent.

The Okavango's warm and slow-moving waters support a rich and varied aquatic life including an exceptional variety of fish. Although the crocodile population has been drastically reduced in recent years, enough still cruise the deeper pools to ensure that human bank-dwellers take no liberties while at the water's edge. The Okavango crocodiles are particularly dangerous during the warm summer months when the river is in full flood and high water temperatures increase the metabolism of these cold-blooded reptiles, which in turn activates their hunger. Hippopotamus once abounded in the Okavango, but over the last two decades uncontrolled hunting has resulted in their virtual extermination from much of the river's extent within Namibia. Besides being prized as a food source they are also persecuted for their forays into maize and millet fields, and occasional attacks on *mukolo* canoes. Today there are probably fewer than fifty hippo left in the 300 kilometre stretch of river between Nkurenkuru and the Botswana border; and whether any will survive the next decade will depend primarily on the successful establishment of a sanctuary somewhere along the river's course. Fortunately proposals for such a sanctuary, south of the Poppa rapids, have recently been accepted by the Kavango authorities.

The planned Okavango River Reserve will not only provide a refuge for hippos and other water-dwelling creatures, but will ensure the preservation of a representative sample of the Okavango's rich riverine vegetation – now threatened, and in places severely degraded, by the rapidly increasing human population along the river's banks. Where this riparian growth is undisturbed, however, there are still magnificent patches of forest fringing the Okavango's deep pools of clear water, creating cool shady vistas.

Only a few kilometres south from the Okavango's banks is a dramatically different world. Here water is the key to survival and from April to November there is little of it available on the surface to sustain man or beast. In this vast region of deep sands and tall tree savannas the only permanent human inhabitants are small bands of nomadic !Kung Bushmen. Only the wiry and sun-wizened !Kung who have no livestock to be watered and can obtain sufficient moisture by sucking the earth with reed pipes, or by squeezing the flesh of wild melons and succulent tubers, can stoically survive the Kalahari's long dry season.

Since time immemorial, the Kavango's Bushmen have set fire to the veld annually, burning off the season's rank grasses and suppressing the regrowth of trees and shrubs. What the Bushmen did not burn was likely to be ignited by fierce electrical storms that danced across the plains at the onset of the rainy season, with the result that up to 90% of the region might burn out in a single year. This fierce fire regime has created some of the finest savanna in Southern Africa, characterised by vigorous perennial grasses growing beneath a light canopy of tall, broad-leaved trees that, once mature, are resistant to the effects of the flames.

Many of the Kavango's larger tree species have considerable economic value, both as a source of traditional veld foods such as the *mangetti* nut and the sweet fruits of the monkey orange tree (*Strychnos* sp.), and for the high quality timber they yield. In the latter role, the renowned kiaat (*Pterocarpus angolensis*) is by far the most valuable, but other species also produce commercially exploitable hardwood. Today a total of 1,8 million hectares of Kavango is designated as forestry land and veld fires are controlled in order to promote a faster regeneration of commercially valuable timber.

When Andersson visited the Kavango in the 1850's, he found more elephants than he had encountered in any other part of Namibia. But a few years later a group of Boer trekkers laid a tragic pattern for wanton slaughter.

Whilst hunting to the south of the Okavango River, Hendrik van Zyl and five companions, including Pieter Botha (who was to become one of Namibia's greatest early hunters), came across a huge herd of elephants, which they chased on horseback into a large swampy vlei. Here the elephants became bogged down, and during the course of the afternoon, the Boers killed every animal — a total of 103 in a single day. During the next two weeks the same party killed a further 75 elephants in this area, collecting over 12 000 lbs of ivory which they subsequently sold in Cape Town for seven shillings a pound. Tales of such hunting successes undoubtedly spurred many young bloods from the Cape Colony to seek their fortunes in Namibia.

After a century of virtually uncontrolled hunting, the wildlife of the Kavango is today but a pale shadow of its former splendour. Nevertheless a number of species survive that did not occur or were shot out in the rest of Namibia. For this reason alone, the creation of conservation areas in this part of the Territory is particulary important and should be undertaken before the vast waterless tracts of sandveld are opened up to cattle ranching by the tapping of the region's substantial subterranean reservoirs.

In a recent Government-sponsored report, a second much larger game reserve in the south-eastern sandveld of this homeland was proposed and has been accepted in principle by the Kavango authorities. The area chosen has outstanding potential, for it comprises both waterless fire-climax savanna and a network of fossil watercourses, the largest of which — the Kaudum — contains scattered permanent vleis. Learning from past mistakes in other areas, the researchers have warned against the development of any artificial waterpoints. Fire should also be retained as an integral part of the reserve management to ensure that natural migrations of grazing game, from the sweet grasslands, along the dry clay-bottomed watercourses, to freshly burned savanna, still takes place at the commencement of each new rainy season. The major managerial problem facing the new reserve will be its size, for in the Kalahari even 3 000 square kilometres falls short of forming a natural ecological unit. However, this could be overcome if it is linked to a similar conserved area in contiguous Bushmanland, and the boundaries of both reserves are not fenced, thus allowing free movement of game into adjoining areas.

Were it not for the ambitions of the 19th century German Chancellor, Count Georg von Caprivi, Namibia would have ended at the Okavango River. Von Caprivi, however, had hopes that German South West Africa might be linked to Tanganyika, another of Germany's African colonies. Although this endeavour was thwarted by Cecil Rhodes, on behalf of the British Empire, the thin strip of land that bears von Caprivi's name has remained a part of Namibia.

Although the Caprivi Strip is nearly 500 kilometres long, much of it is less than 40 kilometres across. This fact has presented considerable administrative problems which are exacerbated by the swampy nature of the soil between the Kwando and Zambesi rivers. The Germans were never able to govern the region effectively, although expeditions were undertaken to the Zambesi, and a small military outpost was eventually established at Schuckmansburg in 1908. After Namibia was mandated to South Africa, the Eastern Caprivi was successively administered from Botswana, Zambia and then directly from Pretoria. It is only since 1980 that Windhoek has played any meaningful role in the Caprivi's affairs — small wonder, since Katima Mulilo, the Caprivi's only town, is over 1 200 kilometres by road from the capital.

The Western Caprivi, lying between the Okavango and Kwando rivers, comprises sandveld savanna little different from much of the Kavango, and during the rainy season large numbers of elephant and a variety of antelope including eland, roan, sable, and tsessebe may be encountered. Lion, cheetah, wild hunting dogs and !Kung Bushman follow in the wake of these nomadic herds. As yet the Caprivi knows no fences — not even along its borders with neighbouring Angola and Botswana — thus allowing both game and Bushmen to wander freely between the three countries, unaffected by veterinary regulations, international protocol and political conflicts.

The Kwando, which forms the divide between Western and Eastern Caprivi, is one of Southern Africa's most unusual waterways. Like all the other major rivers in this area, it rises on the Angolan highlands where it is known as the Kuanza. Soon after cascading down off this plateau, the river meanders slowly through extensive marshlands towards the Zambian border, where it becomes known as the Mashi. It then turns due south and enters the Caprivi Strip approximately 200 kilometres east of the Okavango. At this stage the river, now the Kwando, traverses country so flat that it appears to have no banks at all, its path demarcated merely by a series of deeper and shallower channels that wind sluggishly through beds of tall reeds and lush grassland.

For some forty kilometres the erratic course of the Kwando separates Caprivi from Botswana before finally disappearing altogether into a vast reed and papyrus swamp. Somewhere deep within these swamps the river makes a

sharp turn to the left and, with its name changed to Linyandi, flows north-eastward to where, still in a broad bed of reeds, it eventually empties into Lake Liambezi, the largest sheet of open water in Namibia. The river's long odyssey is not yet over, however, for at the south-east corner of this lake it emerges once more and, after changing its name yet again — this time to the Chobe — it winds leisurely towards the Zambesi, whose waters it joins at Kazangula.

For most of its length the Kwando flows so slowly that its annual flood waters only start reaching the Western Caprivi in late May or June, when both the Okavango and Zambesi rivers are well past their peak flow. This accounts for the extraordinary situation where, at the height of the Zambesi's flood in March and April, its waters may push up the channel of the Chobe, causing this part of the river to flow backwards away from the Zambesi and towards Lake Liambezi.

Liambezi itself has a remarkable history, for less than twenty five years ago there was no lake here at all. Where Liambezi is now situated, a broad shallow depression existed whose rich clay soils had for generations been tilled and planted for crops of millet, sorghum and maize. In 1958 the Zambesi rose to the highest ever recorded floods which not only inundated the entire eastern quarter of East Caprivi — a normal occurrence at this time of the year — but also broke through the high ground between Katima Mulilo and Ngoma, pouring into the Liambezi lowlands, thereby creating the present lake.

Of the East Caprivi's total land surface of 7 200 square kilometres, over 30% is submerged under water at some period during the year. The rest of this region, although part of the Kalahari sandveld system, is criss-crossed by numerous *mulapos* — broad fossil waterways that contain long-lasting and sometimes permanent vleis.

The extensive swamplands of East Caprivi provide a home for a number of animals that occur nowhere else in Namibia and in few other parts of the sub-continent. Among these is the sitatunga, a shy antelope that lives permanently in the very heart of the great reedbeds along the Kwando and Linyandi. The puku, another swamp dweller, is perhaps the rarest antelope in Southern Africa today, occurring only on the Zambesi-Chobe floodplain. During a recent aerial game census only eight of these animals were counted in the Caprivi, and their continued survival here must be regarded as precarious indeed.

Red lechwe, perhaps the most characteristic antelope of the Caprivi swamplands, are still plentiful along the Kwando and Linyandi; but their numbers have decreased drastically on the eastern floodplains from over 16 000 in 1962 to a present estimated total of only 2 000. Hippopotamus still occur in large numbers where human populations are low, and crocodile are found in all the major waterways, being particularly numerous in Lake Liambezi. Away from the floodplains, in the Caprivi's magnificent broad-leaved woodlands and fire-climax savanna, elephant, buffalo and other large game animals are still relatively plentiful, although in recent years the numbers of most species have declined alarmingly.

To a significant extent, the Caprivi's still impressive populations of big game owe their survival to two small insects: the anopheles mosquito and the tsetse fly. Were it not for malaria, sleeping sickness and *nagana*, this fertile region would undoubtedly have been more densely populated by man and his livestock than it is today.

The closely related Fwe and Subia tribes both have well-established systems of tribal chiefs, who have traditionally been responsible for the organisation of hunting parties. Most of the larger game animals were regarded as belonging to the chief and could not be hunted without his permission. Both Caprivi chiefs also retained certain tracts of territory for their sole use.

For the maFwe chiefs, these traditional hunting grounds comprise two islands hidden deep inside the Kwando-Linyandi swamp. Neither Lupala nor Nkasa are islands in the true sense, for both merely comprise a system of high ground set within a vast maze of reed and papyrus with only occasional channels of open water. The virtually impenetrable reed beds that surround these 'islands', and the strict protection afforded by maFwe chiefs, have preserved their pristine character and created a veritable paradise for the wilderness lover.

Seen from the air, Lupala and Nkasa appear as a brilliant mosaic of emerald grasslands sprinkled with graceful palms and stately patches of tall acacial woodland, while everywhere exquisite little pans sparkle in the sun — glittering gems that appear silver, turquoise or deep burgundy according to their depth. Although the combined dry-land area of the two islands is less than 400 square kilometres, they support a remarkable spectrum of big game, including elephant, buffalo, hippo, lion, leopard and great numbers of lechwe.

Human predation has been part of African ecosystems for many millennia, but the instruments of predation have lately changed. On foot with a bow and arrow, man was just another carnivore; with a high-powered rifle and four-wheel-drive vehicle, he is capable of total extermination of large game species within a matter of years. Moreover, the human population of the Kavango alone has grown in the last 20 years from 60 000 to 120 000.

In a tamed world, untamed nature is a marketable commodity. Both the Kavango and Caprivi have enormous tourist appeal if their wild lands remain wild, and filled with game. The parched Kalahari sands in fact do not have much other potential: in such an area nature conservation is no longer a luxury, it is as important as medical and educational services. If undertaken with both ecological and human sensitivity, the economic spin-off from a healthy natural environment could make a valuable contribution towards the well-being of all sections of the population.

181

Above: An unnamed stream
near Ruacana swollen by
heavy rains.

Below: *Adenium boehmianum,* a beautiful
flowering succulent.

Opposite: At Ruacana
the Kunene plunges into a deep
gorge in a profusion of cascades.

Previous pages:
North of Etosha,
meandering channels of
the seasonally flooded
Ekuma River
weave complex patterns
through a
flattened landscape.

Dusk in Ovamboland.

At the climax of the rainy season,
Ovamboland presents a picture of water
in extravagant abundance.
Flooded pans known as *oshanas*
are everywhere in evidence,
providing a rich habitat
for fish- and plant-life, such as
the waterlily (*Nymphaea lotus*) below.

Overleaf top: At sunset
makalani palms (*Hyphaene ventricosa*) and a
towering termite mound are
thrown into sharp relief.

Overleaf below: Hippopotamus,
once prolific in all the northern waterways,
today face an uncertain future
in the Okavango.

Top:
*Lonchocarpus
capassa,* a common
tree species
in the vicinity of
the Okavango River.
Its green wood
is used for the
construction of
mukolo canoes.

Below:
A sub-adult bullfrog;
*Pyxicephalus
adspersus.*

Opposite:
Poppa rapids on the
Okavango River.

Left: The Chobe flood plain in Eastern Caprivi provides perfect habitat for a pair of fish eagles.

Centre, above: Sacred Ibis displaying a classic formation in flight.

Below: A carmine bee-eater pauses momentarily from feeding. Its prey consists of small beetles, grasshoppers and flying insects which are skilfully caught in mid-air.

Above: Awkward and ungainly in appearance, the Marabou stork is nevertheless an efficient scavenger in the African veld, and fulfils an important role in the ecosystem.

Left: Scattered plants
of hibiscus *(H. diversifolius*
subspecies *rivularis)*
give a splash of
vibrant colour to the
swampy shores of
Lake Lisikili in
Eastern Caprivi.

Overleaf:
Western Caprivi consists
of a seemingly
endless plain of
woodland savanna.

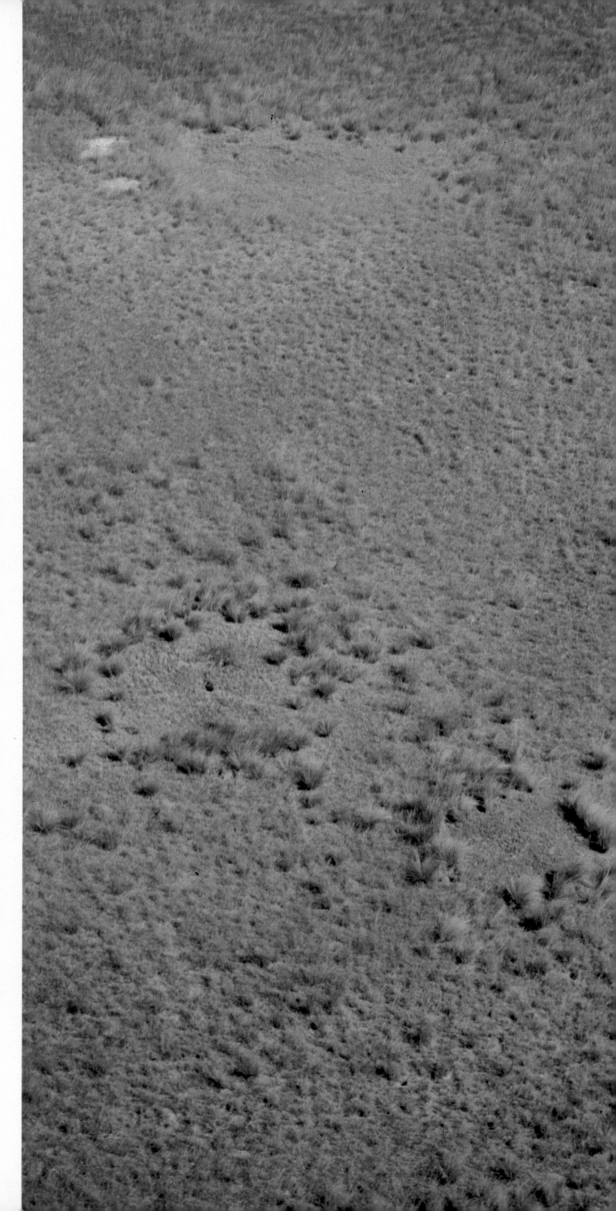

A herd of plains zebra
moves across
the flood plain in
Eastern Caprivi.

Previous pages:
Left, above:
Clerodendrum spinescens

Left, below:
Blister beetle *(Mylabris* sp.*)*

Centre, above:
A python creeper *(Fockea* sp.*)*
twists tightly around
the trunk of
its host.

Centre, below:
Hibiscus diversifolius
subspecies *rivularis*

Right: In parts of Africa
red velvet mites
are known as 'rain beetles'
due to their frequent
appearance after rainfall.

Following pages:
Lake Liambizi, into
which the Linyandi River
disappears, to emerge
once again in the east
as the Chobe River.

The annual floods
of the mighty Zambesi
dictate the ecological
destiny of much
of Eastern Caprivi.

Sunset over the Zambesi.